W9-BMU-730

Music, Saddles & Flapjacks

Dudes at the OTO Ranch

*Roberta Cheney
and Clyde Erskine*

2000
MOUNTAIN PRESS PUBLISHING COMPANY
Missoula, Montana

PICTURE CREDITS

UM: University of Montana Archives

Museum of the Rockies: courtesy of
Margaret Wood, curator and friend of the OTO Ranch.

All other photographs: courtesy of Clyde Erskine and the OTO Ranch.

Second Edition, June 2000

Library of Congress Cataloging-in-Publication Data
Cheney, Roberta Carkeek.
    Music, saddles & flapjacks : dudes at the OTO Ranch / Roberta
Cheney and Clyde Erskine.—2nd ed.
    p. cm.
    ISBN 0-87842-422-9 (alk. paper)
    1. Randall, Dick. 2. Dude ranchers—Montana—Biography.
3. OTO Ranch. I. Title: Music, saddles and flapjacks. II. Erskine,
Clyde. III. Title.
TX910.5.R35 C43 2000
647.94786'092—dc21
[B]   00–040104

Mountain Press Publishing Company
P. O. Box 2399 • Missoula, MT 59806
(406) 728-1900 • email: mtnpress@montana.com

To Bess Randall Erskine and to the memory of Mother Randall, two women who pioneered with their men in all phases of the dude ranch business.

CONTENTS

INTRODUCTION

"If, after you've spent a month on a Montana Ranch, riding horseback every day and being outdoors, you don't feel better—you don't need a doctor, you need an undertaker and there's no hope for you."
— Dick Randall

This is the story of Dick Randall, his family and the OTO Dude Ranch on Cedar Creek near Yellowstone National Park. The 3,000-acre ranch is bound on three sides by the Absaroka-Beartooth Wilderness and is home to elk, whitetail and mule deer, black and grizzly bear, wolves, mountain lions, coyotes, game and song birds and many other species of Montana wildlife.

In about 1912, Montana ranchers began to take in hunting guests and naturalists. Dude ranching came into its prime during this early period, and Dick Randall was one of the first dude ranchers in the state. OTO guests came from Germany, England, Scotland and all parts of the United States. Trains brought them to Montana, and the Randalls met them at the train station in Corwin Springs with four-horse teams. Most guests stayed all summer. Upon arrival, each dude was assigned a horse that was his or hers for as long as he or she was at the OTO.

By the late 1930s, the stock market crash of 1929 and the ensuing depression had taken their toll on dude ranches in Montana and other western states. The OTO passed out of Randall's hands and for some years was a cattle ranch, operating into the 1940s. It was then sold and resold, and over time the buildings fell into disrepair.

In 1991, the Gallatin National Forest acquired the historic OTO Ranch. With the help of the Rocky Mountain Elk Foundation, which expended tremendous effort and the necessary financial support, the U.S. Forest Service assumed ownership of the OTO Ranch. In October 1992, the Forest Service presented several alternatives for the preservation of the historic property at a public planning meeting. This planning continues to guide the present management of the OTO.

With the strong support and concurrence of the Montana Historical Society, the OTO has been nominated to the National Register of Historic Places. Restoration and stabilization of the ranch buildings and work on the landscape began in 1997. In the following years, dozens of volunteers accomplished significant historic restoration: They added new roofs to ten cabins, replaced bad logs, fixed and rehung windows and doors, replaced problem floors and nearly completed the earthwork around the cabins. The volunteers cleaned the lodge and some of the other buildings and collected, sorted and stored the contents. They constructed a jack-leg fence to define the historic building site, hung a new gate, graded and partially graveled the road and built a new bridge over Cedar Creek. Work has been done on acres of brush and weed, and miles of wire fencing has been removed to facilitate wildlife movement.

With the generous aid of individual volunteers and volunteer groups who are working side by side with Forest Service leaders, the historic building restoration continues as does work on the land itself. Many of these volunteer restorers have come through Amizade, Inc., a nonprofit foundation out of Chicago. Others have come through Forest Service–sponsored programs at the OTO such as the Passport in Time Volunteer Project and the Heritage Expedition Project. Some volunteers will come from the Elderhostel program and other groups. The Forest Service plans to restore and preserve the thirty-odd buildings and bring the grounds back to the original condition, so that the OTO once again may be enjoyed by everyone.

All visitors and volunteers are welcome to join one of the work sessions, just come and visit the ranch, or sign up to receive the OTO Newsletter. Contact the Gardiner Ranger District, P.O. Box 5, Gardiner, Montana 59030; telephone (406) 848-7375; e-mail wgoutermont@fs.fed.us.

Work on this restoration requires little or no specialized training. Volunteers need only have a zest for the outdoors, a spirit for hard work and the desire to help restore an important part of our past. Today, people return to the OTO as participants—solving problems, working toward common goals, and becoming friends while they learn about each other and the past. They are coming to the OTO to work, to refresh their spirits, to forget their troubles—and to avoid both the doctor and the undertaker.

So, let us turn back to a more rugged and perhaps romantic time of the early OTO and read of its development and its people. This book is not meant to be a biography or a chronological history of the ranch. Rather, it gives the reader glimpses into the people and events that led to the development of Montana's first dude ranch and shows the unique and warm relationship that grew between Dick Randall and his guests. Whenever possible, we let Dick tell his own stories and hope the reader will catch the personal magnetism of this man who, for many years, held campfire and lodge audiences spellbound as he related pioneering and hunting experiences.

This book is a joint effort of Clyde Erskine and Roberta Cheney. Clyde, the son-in-law of Dick Randall, furnished the materials: photos, newspaper clippings, magazine articles, brochures, Dick's unpublished memoirs and Clyde's own reminiscences. Roberta edited and organized these materials and wrote explanatory passages. For prefatory information concerning the Forest Service ownership, the volunteers and the restoration, we are gratefully indebted to Wayne Goutermont of the U.S. Forest Service; Ron Gardner, head of the Gardiner Ranger District; and Walt Allen of the Historical Preservation Office of the Bozeman Ranger District.

ROBERTA CHENEY
March, 2000

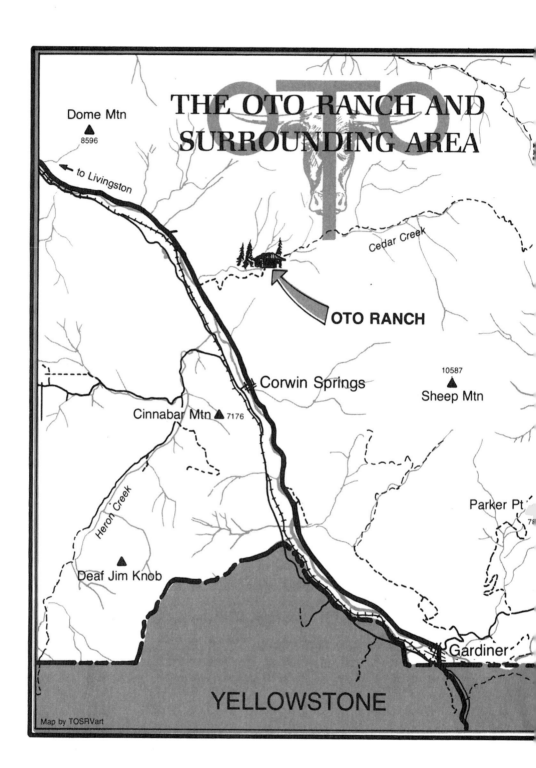

THE OTO RANCH AND SURROUNDING AREA

Dome Mtn
▲
8596

← to Livingston

Cedar Creek

OTO RANCH

Corwin Springs

10587
▲
Sheep Mtn

Cinnabar Mtn ▲ 7176

Heron Creek

Parker Pt
78

▲
Deaf Jim Knob

Gardiner

YELLOWSTONE

Map by TOSRVart

x

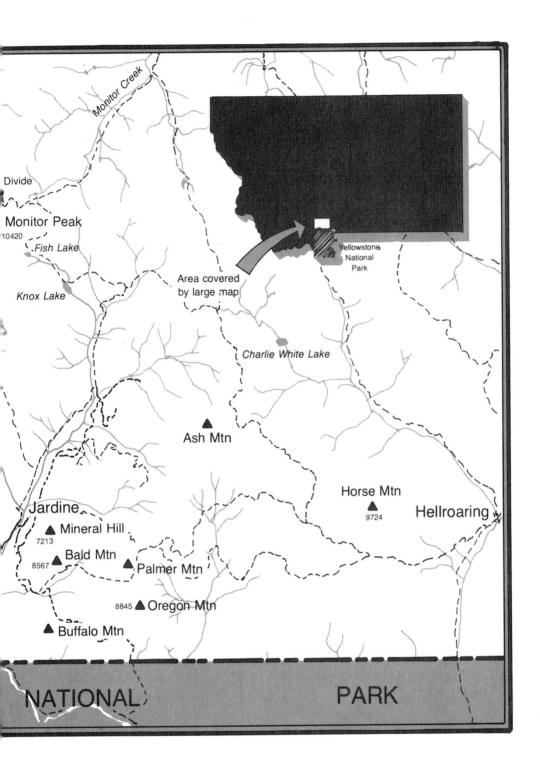

Divide

Monitor Peak
10420

Fish Lake

Knox Lake

Monitor Creek

Area covered
by large map

Yellowstone
National
Park

Charlie White Lake

▲
Ash Mtn

Horse Mtn
▲
9724

Jardine
▲ Mineral Hill
7213

Hellroaring

▲ Bald Mtn
8567   ▲ Palmer Mtn

8845 ▲ Oregon Mtn

▲ Buffalo Mtn

NATIONAL   PARK

LORD BLAKE AND
THE GRIZZLIES

In between the raucous era of prospectors, gold miners, and Vigilantes, and the era of energy battles for coal and water, there was a romantic period in Montana's history. Wealthy Easterners and European royalty went Western. They came in increasing numbers to spend summers in an Old West atmosphere. Dude Ranching began in Montana about 1912 and reached its peak of popularity about a decade later.

This is the story of Dick Randall and his OTO Ranch. Dick is recognized as the first dude rancher in Montana, and had what it took to be a successful one. He was equally at home with Yellowstone Park stage drivers, cussing an eight-horse team or with Lord and Lady Blake from England. He charmed all with stories of earlier days: lion hunts in Yellowstone, riding fenceless Montana ranges and cattle herds numbering to 40,000 head.

"Have you told them the one about shooting the five grizzlies?" Lord Blake asked as they sat around the Lodge fireplace one evening several years after that particular hunt.

"No, but you start it out, and I'll finish. We had some real excitement on that trip." Dick leaned back, lighted his pipe and the guests knew he was chuckling inside — the way he always did getting ready to tell a story.

"Well, you see," said the Lord from Castle Cary, "Someone told me the greatest challenge to any hunter is a wounded grizzly, so I decided I wanted that experience. The Governor, here, didn't think much of the idea, but he's a good guide and anxious to please, so he set the whole thing up.

"We packed the camp equipment and headed for the mountains. Dick brought along an old crippled work horse to use for bait. He killed the horse at the spot where he wanted to set the trap, then put the trap at the rear of the carcass and built a camouflage of brush and logs. It was interesting to watch Dick make the trap. He put squirrel manure on his gloves to kill human scent, then took out a chain about eight feet long. He cut off the end of a log and ran the small end through a ring on the chain, driving it into the ground as far as he could, splitting the log and driving a wedge into it, thus holding it securely.

"The most dangerous bear, he told me, is one dragging a trap, so you want to be sure he can't pull up the stake. Dick set the spring on the trap and backed away very carefully so as not to snap it.

" 'Need to let that bait ripen for about ten days,' he says. 'We'll go on into the higher mountains and look for mountain sheep — should be about right when we get back.' Dick figured the rotting carcass would scent the mountain air and attract bears during that ten days. Well, he was right!

"We arrived back at this campsite one evening. I was anxious to go look at the trap. Dick warned me to be careful not to let the bears get wind of me, and to only go as far as the place he had pointed out to me.

"Randall set about making camp and building a fire; I went toward the trap. In a few minutes, I came running back. 'Dick! We got one.' The two of us went to the spot selected earlier as a good vantage point from which we could shoot. It was about 35 yards from the carcass and there was a clearing between so we would have a good shot to make the kill. When we got there, we saw a two-year old grizzly near the log trap. Dick whispered to be sure my Carbine was fully loaded. He looked my gun over, then gave the word: 'Go ahead and shoot. *Now*, Blake.'

"I did, and all Hell broke loose; grizzly bears appeared from everywhere. I could feel the earth tremble and I lost my head. I quit right there, Dick, and I felt that if ever a man let his friend down, I did it then. Now you take over the story, Dick."

"Yes, sir, that was quite a predicament," Dick continued the yarn. "I knew we had gotten into a family affair...a bear family, that is. His Highness, here...I called him that even though he often said, 'Just call me Edward or Blake and forget that fancy handle when we're in America.'

"Well," Dick continued, "His Highness was pumping shells out of his gun. I hollered for him to keep those shells in and to put more in whenever he had time. I knew we were going to be busy for awhile and might need every shell. Next thing I knew, I looked up and Blake had disappeared. I began to size up the situation. There was a two year old grizzly in the trap. He was crying so loud it threw the other bears off balance; they couldn't locate exactly where the shooting was coming from, so I was able to take them one at a time. The next one to come in sight was the old boar and he was a mighty big grizzly. I shot and knocked him down three times. Each time he got up, he came toward me. He got within six feet of me before he finally fell. I put the mother bear down with two shots and two younger bears with one shot each...happened to hit right through the heart. The one in the trap wasn't dangerous, so I left him to last. He hadn't been able to pull up the log and chain and was crying and fighting the trap when I pulled up on him.

"When I got back to camp, there stood Blake with a six shooter in his hand. He offered the gun to me and said, 'Now finish the job; shoot me, too. I sure did let you down.'

" 'No need to do that, Your Highness,' I said, 'but what do you think of the guy that told you it would be good sport to meet a wounded grizzly?' "

Lord Blake who had been listening and reminiscing about this and other hunts with Randall, spoke up to finish the story. "I said that guy might have killed a lion, but he sure as hell never met a wounded grizzly."

Dick Randall didn't start out to be a Dude Rancher. The idea and development of the first Dude Ranch in Montana grew out of his association with Easterners and foreigners who wanted guides on hunting trips.

*"I was in the big game hunting business. We were trying to make a living. I'd have a hunter out who had some children and maybe the next summer the family was going abroad, and we'd take on the children because I'd been out with the parents big game hunting. So the next year, they'd come back and bring two or three with them, so that my wife and I would have to sleep in a tent, giving up our bed, we had so darn many guests. Not any of them paying guests at first. We would just give them a saddle horse and let them go. We had a log house with a dirt roof. Then, because there got to be so many guests, we began building cabins to take care of them and charging for our protection. But the Dude Ranch business sprang up from just trying to be a good fellow; most of it anyway.

"Theodore Roosevelt came West for his health, bought a ranch right next to the Eatons. The Eaton brothers, Howard, Alden, and Willis had the same problem with guests over at their North Dakota place, so they started charging and then set up a paying guest ranch in Wyoming. Roosevelt was made sheriff of the county he lived in, and he had his deputies; old Bill Jones was one of them. I was his big game guide when he used to come up from Medora for a hunt. Later on Bill Jones worked for me as a packer and guide. I was with Roosevelt on several big game trips. The last one I took them on, there were four of them: Roosevelt, Colonel Appleton, Phillip Ashton Rawlins, the writer, and a Dr. Fuller.

"Once I made a trip with a big steel man's son. Had him out for a 60 day trip. He had five servants with him. On a hunting trip, you don't need servants, but he insisted. He also brought along his doctor and it took one extra pack horse to carry the medical case and the surgical case they had. That young man didn't have any chance for a feel of the West and freedom with all that retinue along.

"Another time, I took Hartly Dodge, Jr. on a bear hunting trip. We got seven. Hartley was the only son of Geraldine Rockefeller Dodge, William Rockefeller's daughter and she was worth about 150 million, I guess. I was in Cleveland when she hired me to take her son

---

* All first person accounts by Dick Randall are taken from his Memoirs, a notebook full of unpublished material.

4

Dick and Dora were married on Thanksgiving Day in Helena.
The ceremony and special wedding dinner were at the old Placer Hotel.

June Buzzell in authentic clothes of an early-day Montana cowboy. "There was only one pocketbook between him and me," Dick Randall said in describing their partnership.

Yellowstone Park Transportation Company coach. Dick Randall drove this one between Gardiner and Mammoth Hot Springs. Many of the friends he made on these guided tours around the park came back in the fall to go on hunting trips with him.

In later years, Dick Randall posed with one of the dudes in the driver's seat of an old Yellowstone Park coach.

Dick Randall in 1890. Photo by his friend F.J. Haynes, official Yellowstone Park photographer, was taken where the Mammoth Hotel was later built.
—Museum of the Rockies 89.36.21

Dora Randall driving her favorite horse, Black Beauty, into the Gardiner entrance to Yellowstone Park.

Dick Randall (right) and his hunting partner, Bill Vinson of Ottuma, Iowa, had just returned from a hunt and were met in Mammoth by Dora and the children who had driven the Surrey the seventeen miles from the ranch and insisted upon a family picture. Taken at the Haynes Studio in Mammoth January 14, 1901. —UM

"Mitchell and Payton wanted trophy heads and we found plenty of old bull elk with huge racks of horns. The life of an elk is about eight years. The old ones often winter kill."

We got permission to hunt on the Flathead Indian reservation.
Indian cowboys went with us to be sure we took care of any animal we shot.
Hunters from Scotland and Jamaica took the heads and we gave the meat to the Indians.

After their return to Scotland, Mitchell and Payton sent this photo with an album of snapshots of the hunting trip they had taken with Dick.

This was the beginning of the OTO. In 1898, Dick Randall bought a one room cabin (with porch) from a couple of stage coach robbers who had to be "movin' on". He added two sections but the house still couldn't accommodate the people that came by to "go hunting with Dick."

F.J. Haynes (right) bound for Canyon of the Yellowstone. Camera on sled drawn by horse named Rock.

Dick Randall just back from a hunting trip wearing his all leather suit.

Dick Randall was convinced that a good pack trip into the high country could cure Wall Street nerves. Photo courtesy of George Randall.

Cutting out horses to be used on a fall hunting trip from the OTO. The old homestead cabin in the background was once a robber's hideout. Photo courtesy of Gay Randall.

Dick Randall, left, the camp cook, Wes Ritchie, and June Buzzell organized and guided the famous Von Hindenburg hunting trip.

The package for Bess from a lady in Philadelphia turned out to be a fine Ludwig piano. Dick hauled it home in a dead-axe wagon over steep mountain roads.

There was great excitement when the big crate arrived safely at the ranch. Bess and her brother perch on top of it for a picture.

Howard Eaton, pioneer dude rancher in Wyoming, meets with OTO dudes in Yellowstone Park. Bess Randall Erskine is second from the left and Howard Eaton is next to her.

All furniture for the cabins and the lodge was made on the ranch. —UM

Pat and Gail Randall, third generation dude wranglers. —UM

*A pole bridge spanned Cedar Creek between the cabins and the saddle room.
Dudes waiting for their horses line up for a photo.*

Bess Erskine and her favorite horse, Flip, survey the valley below.

Clyde in his purple velvet shirt all dressed up for the "dudes."

hunting. He was a Princeton student and crazy about the West. Everybody liked him and I will say that Hartley Dodge Jr. was one of the best millionaire's sons I ever hunted with. I'll write more about him later on."

COWBOYS AND INDIANS

James Norris (Dick) Randall was born June 10, 1866 at Birmingham, Van Buren County, Iowa. He ran away from home at the age of twelve and after a few years working in a packing plant in Ottumwa, headed for the West and adventure. An older brother, Billy, had settled at old Junction City, Montana. Dick landed in Miles City and met up with Paul McCormick, who managed the 7 Bar 7 outfit, and started to work for him.

"Paul McCormick was the manager; T. C. Powers of Helena and Dan Floweree were the fellows that had the money and owned the cattle. We were rangin' the cattle east of Billings and down around the old town of Junction City. We ranged from the Yellowstone over to the Musselshell, ran about 50,000 head of cattle, scattered plumb into the Powder River country. This outfit would buy out other brands; the O Z was one they bought.

"Junction City was right in sight of where the Custer battle was fought. All cow camp supplies came from Junction City. Paul McCormick owned the big store there; we all thought he was the biggest man around. He would start out with a pocket full of silver dollars whenever he rode across the Reservation. Every time he met an Indian, a squaw especially, he'd slip her a dollar. That's how he got along. He could get anything he wanted on the Reservation.

"At the time, Nelson Story over at Bozeman was trying to break in, but Paul McCormick was too heavy for him. Story had a lot of cattle and the Crow Reservation was the cream of Montana range. But Paul was too foxy; he had the Indians bought, so Story couldn't get in. McCormick ran in the Shields River Valley, too; he ran his cattle all over Eastern Montana. This country all belonged to the Crows then; their agency was here on Mission Creek. The government kept cutting off slices of Crow country.

"Right up here at Emigrant there is a buffalo jump. The buffalo would come up from the plains country. There would be stringers or tail-enders that wouldn't go over the rock cliffs, so they would pile up and then the Indians would shoot them with bows and arrows. I have an island here on my place, the Yellowstone on one side and Spring Creek on the other where there are lots of Indian graves. I say let them rest. Some people want to get anything that might be around for curios, but I say let them be. Came across a boy once with a whole cart full of arrow-heads; guess he had been diggin' in the graves."

Randall was an outdoorsman and a hunter. He had great respect for nature and the scheme of wild life as it was. He loved the mountains and knew every animal that inhabited his section of the Rockies. He knew every trail and camp site, where the best hunting was, and how to do it.

The winter of 1887 and '88, Dick and June Buzzell had moved in with an old trapper and hunter who liked to tell in detail of his experiences. He would tell all the fine points of how to hunt and the habits of the big game animals. He even made maps of the area and marked the good camp sites, ones near water and with meadows for the horses. Dick listened and learned. He added that knowledge to what he had gained from his own experiences in the mountains. Dick and June put together their own pack outfit and guided hunters who came from out-of-state.

Once Dick had a man by the name of Scott out in the mountains. Scott wanted to get a large grizzly. The snow was deep and it was hard going. They had been hunting for several hours, following a bear track. All of a sudden they could see that a big grizzly had crossed over the track they were following. Dick knew it was a fresh track and told Scott not to follow in the track, but to stay as far away from it as possible without losing sight of it.

"Load your saddle carbine and start out, but watch those tracks," Dick instructed as he went on the opposite side of the tracks and was careful to stay a little behind, so Scott would jump the grizzly first.

About thirty minutes after the two men separated, Scott looked up the side of the mountain and there was the grizzly. He leveled his rifle at the broad chest as the animal reared full length, glaring at him. The bear dropped his front legs to his side, waiting for his opponent to make a move. Scott fired. The bear was coming toward him; Scott never took the rifle from his shoulders; he just kept firing. Dick heard the shots and rushed over to him, thinking that Scott must have lost his head. When Dick reached Scott, he was lying on the ground and Dick was afraid the grizzly had gotten to him. But when he looked closer, Dick saw the dead bear was still six feet from Scott and had not touched him. The bear's vital organs were all shot away. Dick put snow on Scott's face and he finally came to; he had just fainted.

"Scott had shot a big, beautiful trophy and he was really happy."

Dick met up with June Buzzell at the 7 Bar 7, and they hit it off together, riding in the summer, batching in the winter. They rode the line protecting McCormick's interests. Cowmen of those days made no provision for winter feed, other than natural winter forage. There was no shelter except what the cattle could find in deep coulees or the lee of rimrocks. The job of the two young cowboys was to keep the cattle from bunching up under the rimrocks lest they smother each other in a storm. They were also supposed to get the animals out where they could forage if there was any grass in sight. The hard winter of 1886 took a lot of cattle. Charlie Russell described it with his famous picture "The Last of the 5,000." That winter, Dick and June realized the day of herding for big outfits was over, so they started planning their future. In the spring they decided to buy a string of horses from the Indians and start a pack outfit.

"We went to Gardiner and started big game hunting. June and I lived in a cabin there. Him and I had punched cows as young fellers in eastern Montana. There was only one pocketbook between us. After the hard winter of 1886, the cow punching business was off because every cow man in the country lost so many cattle; most of them went broke. June and I bought 80 head of horses from the Indians and we brought them overland to Yellowstone National Park in the spring of 1887. The government had no pack trains then."

The story of how Dick and June made the horse deal and got the herd to Gardiner was a favorite one with Dudes in future years when the OTO was entertaining guests from all parts of the world.

"It was in the spring of '87 right after that hard winter that my partner and I started out to buy a string of horses from the Indians, figuring we could put together a pack string and hire out to government workers in the Park and to hunting parties. We went over to the Reservation; June bought a beautiful buckskin gelding from the Chief; then we kept on buying more horses. 'Bout a week before we were figuring to start for the Yellowstone with our string, this gelding came up missing. An Indian that was especially friendly with us said an Indian renegade had the horse locked up in a kind of lean-to he had built on his tepee.

"Now, you have to realize that an Indian's idea of horse dealin' ain't quite the same as ours. Horse stealin' was a game they played, so we couldn't just go claim the horse by saying we had bought it. We made plans as to how we'd get that horse back. I was to go into the tepee and pow-wow with this Indian renegade. I was to sit next to him on a buffalo robe, and I figured he'd be proud of it and glad to have me talk about it, and I could get a corner of it worked out to the edge of the tepee. June was to be on the outside of the tepee with a rope that he could tie onto a corner of the robe. When I gave the robe a jerk, that was the signal for June to bust the horse out of the lean-to and start gallopin'. He got it tied all right, and I jerked the robe and jumped up, ran out of the tepee and onto my horse and started for the river. When I looked back, there was June on his gelding still hanging onto the rope. The buffalo robe and the whole tepee was trailin' along behind. The Indian had got mixed up in the ropes and had a hard time getting loose. Old June almost got more than he bargained for that time, because by then the other Indians in the village were yelling, and they started shooting at us. June had to duck the fire by crouching down on the far side of his horse.

"When he got to the river where I was, we gathered the rest of the horses corraled there and headed west along the Yellowstone fast as we could go.

"We had to cross the river and up by Columbus there was a fella named Countryman who had a ferry. He wanted four-bits a head to ferry the horses across the river and we didn't have that much money left, so we had to ford the river. Gettin' that many horses to swim the Yellowstone when it was high water in the spring was quite an undertaking. The water was high, muddy and rollin' fast. There was an island in the middle of the river, so we jumped the horses in, got them to swim to the island, rest awhile and then swim on to the other shore.

"We had to get them rounded up and then travel fast, because the Indians were still after us. Finally they quit chasing us; anyway, we couldn't hear them yellin' anymore, so we slowed down our pace a little.

"We still couldn't afford to dally, though, in case some of those Indians decided to come and take back some of our horses. So the next day, we rode and drove those horses clear to the Boulder River; took us 24 hours straight traveling. We laid over two days at Big Timber. I was still worried the Indians might catch up with us but June said, no, he was sure we were safe now. June had some Indian blood in his veins and he knew them better than I did, so I took his word for it.

"Well, the Indians back where we bought the horses didn't come, but I had other Indian trouble. There was a village right outside Big Timber and June fell for a pretty Indian girl. I couldn't get him to move out of that village and I was still nervous about being followed. I knew if they once caught up with us, it would be mud for both of us. As I said, Indians don't understand about buying horses; they think it is great sport and great honor to steal a herd.

"After two days, I finally got June moving again and we drove the horses to Decker flat where we put our brand on them. We got to know those horses pretty well on that drive and we could spot the good ones. We were breaking horses all along the way. We'd rope and throw a saddle on a different one each day. So when we got back to Gardiner, we picked out some of the best ones to keep for our riding string and turned the rest out in a pasture near Mt. Everts. That mountain was named for Truman Everts. He was with the Washburn party in 1870 and got lost. It was 37 days before they found him. He'd been living on grasshoppers and was pretty weak. It was Jack Burnett found him and Jack shot a mountain lion right near him.

"June and I went to Mammoth Hot Springs and contacted George Wakefield to get a job. He hired me as night herder at Old Faithful and put June on at Canyon. We were to take care of the transportation company's stage horses. Now, when you're working at Old Faithful, you don't need an alarm clock. Every night I'd hobble one horse with my lariat rope; then I'd lie down on the edge of the cone and go to sleep. When the geyser began to rumble, I'd go check on the horses. That way I looked at them every hour."

One morning Dick found the horses had strayed. What he had thought were horses in the distance were just white formations that loomed up in the darkness during the night. He was late getting the horses into the corral that day. Wakefield was upset; the stages would be late getting out. "If that pretty Dick Randall doesn't get here with those horses pretty soon, he'll be going down the road." There were five or six other "Dicks" working for Wakefield at that time and from then on, in that territory, Randall was known as "pretty Dick". In 1922 a letter from a lady in England came addressed to "Pretty Dick, Yellowstone Park, Wyoming" and it was delivered. She had made a trip throught the Park with Dick back in 1887. At that time Chet Lindsay was a lieutenant in the army stationed in Yellowstone Park, and in 1922 he happened to be postmaster at Mammoth Hot Springs, so he sent the letter on to the OTO Ranch.

Dick started driving stage for Wakefield in Yellowstone Park and each summer he worked there and then took hunters out in the winter. Often his stage passengers came back for hunting. Dick and June also got many of their hunters through the Army Post. The government men recognized that these men knew the territory of Wyoming, Montana, and Idaho and could always get the best of trophies for hunters they guided. They could almost guarantee deer, bear, elk, or whatever the hunters wanted.

EARLY TRAIL RIDERS

Dora Roseborough had come with her family from Kansas to settle on a ranch in the Deer Lodge Valley of Montana. Dora, then sixteen, had already taught a year in a Kansas rural school. She was the oldest girl in a family of eight children. Her father tried farming in the Valley for two years. It was hard work for all the family and still they couldn't make a living. Mr. Roseborough's brother ran a stage station at Soda Butte in Yellowstone Park half way between Gardiner and Cooke City. He persuaded Logan Roseborough to bring his family and come to the Park where lots of jobs were opening up. They came, and it was in Gardiner that Dora met Dick Randall.

"They were a dashing couple," recalled a friend. Both liked fine horses and Dick had a matching team they used for surrey rides." Dora loved to dance; Dick didn't dance, but he took her to all the dances and in due time they became engaged.

Years later Dick recalled the time he had been out on a hunting trip with his pack train. When he returned to Gardiner, he immediately tied up his horses, still loaded with the kill. This was something he had never done before since he always took care of his horses first. He rushed to see Dora, in spite of not having shaved for a month. She wouldn't kiss him, so he went to his little shack, unpacked the horses, fed them, went in and shaved, took his old buckskin outift off and after cleaning up went back for that kiss.

Not too long after that, they started for Helena to get married. About half way between Gardiner and Livingston the train broke down. It was cold; there was no heat in the cars and the young couple along with other passengers had to spend the night stalled on the tracks. Later they made it to Helena and were married on Thanksgiving Day, 1892.

Dick brought his bride back to Gardiner and to the little log house overlooking the Yellowstone River. Their next door neighbor was Calamity Jane, who lived there for five years. The Randall's first child was a son, Lesley Watson (Gay) and he loved to visit Calamity. She gave him cookies and would kiss him and make over him. She loved children, but this close affection worried Mrs. Randall and she would scrub her son's mouth with homemade yellow soap fearing he would get "some bad disease" from Calamity Jane. Gay loved those cookies and whenever he could run away, he went back to Calamity's for more treats.

It was later that Dick rode into Cedar Creek and bought the ranch. He had been elk hunting in this valley where a clear stream made its way between evergreen trees. Dick noticed a little shack on the side of the mountain with smoke pouring out of the chimney. Wondering who was living there, he rode up to the cabin and knocked on the door. He recognized the man who came to the door as *Al Johns, who had been one of his packers on a hunting trip. Dick tied his pony to a post and went into the cabin. He gradually came to realize that Al was now a partner with Ben Turner and that they were the men who had been robbing the Yellowstone Park stage coaches. Undoubtedly, this was a robber's hideout, but Dick just went on talking about the pack trips they had been on together, until Al said, "What do you think about this little valley Ben and I have Squatters Rights on?"

"It's beautiful, Al. I wish I could find a place like this for my horses."

"I'll sell it to you, Dick, I'm movin' on."

Never one to procrastinate, Randall said, "I'll buy everything you have — horses, packs, and equipment, and I'll bring you the money tomorrow morning." They settled on a price and in a ten-minute transaction, Dick bought the place that was to develop into the OTO Dude Ranch. He rode away a happy man; now able to have a place of his own. As Dick started off down the trail, Al called after him, "Tell Mrs. Randall her jars are all here, but they're empty."

_____

* Fictitious names have been used here.

14

Dick knew for sure then these were the men who had robbed the Yellowstone stage coaches and the ones who had taken things from Mrs. Randall's cellar. They hadn't dared show their faces on the streets of Gardiner, so couldn't buy groceries. They survived the winter on wild game, along with canned fruits and vegetables from the Randall's root cellar.

"I liked the look of Cedar Creek, twelve miles from the Gardiner entrance of the Park. Mrs. Randall proved up on a half-section and I took a half section; that was in 1898. The National Park had been created in 1872, but the government hadn't spent any money in there yet. A few citizens and a few natives lived in the area. In 1884 a troop of Cavalry was stationed in the Park.

"Later on when visitors began to come to the Park, a stage line was set up. Every morning the stage went to Norris Basin and changed horses; then on to Lower Geyser basin where they changed horses again. At Upper Geyser Basin, they stayed all night. The stage travelled a mountain road that had just been cleared and every driver had to carry an axe in case he had to hack away fallen trees. They had to have a night man to herd the stage stock and there wasn't any corral to hold the horses. I had that job one summer and it wasn't easy. If something spooked the horses and they stampeded, it was hard to keep them away from the geysers.

"June and I had those 80 head of horses and we had to find some work for them. The government had cavalry troops and one pack mule for the whole outfit, so we began working for them. I had to earn some money so I could start building up my ranch. Surveyors began to come into the Park and we got jobs furnishing pack outfits and guiding. Lt. Craighill was in charge of the survey of Upper Geyser Basin over the Continental divide and his assigned area ended at Inspiration Point.

"About the time the government started to approach me for horses, they also sent in the Fish Commissioners: Professor Jordan, Professor Spangler, and Professor Gilbert from Washington D.C. We spent one summer seining every stream and every lake in Yellowstone Park for specimens of feed and species of fish. One horse was loaded with two copper cans of alcohol. When a prof got a specimen he wanted, he put it in one of those cans. We always figured in the early days that warm water was the cause of wormy fish in Yellowstone Lake and Heart Lake. Jordan exploded that theory. He found that hot water had nothing to do with it; it was the droppings from pelicans, gulls and swan that led to wormy fish. We stocked the Fire Hole river with Loch Laven and Dolly Varden trout. We stocked Nez Perce Creek and Spring Creek, too, and these streams proved the old professor was right."

Randall became an expert on fish and fishing and part of the popularity of his OTO ranch was that he kept the streams well stocked with fish and he helped many a Dude learn to catch them.

"There're an awful lot of people that played a prominent part here in the West as trail blazers. They never got any credit; went through a lot of heart aches. A few of them got a little glory but most didn't.

"There was Cooke City and the New World Mining district right over near the northwest corner of the Park. The discoverer of the Cooke City ore was Bart Henderson, along with Horn Miller and Pike Moore. Those three went across the plains in the early days and on the '49 Gold Rush to California. They drifted back to Virginia City and finally here to the Yellowstone and set up camp on what they later named Miller Creek after old Horn.

"Old Horn Miller lived with me for a number of winters. In the early days, these big wagon trains started out of Missouri down around St. Louis. Horn had come through with the early settlers and then drifted back to the Yellowstone country. He had one of those big powder horns, and he was from Pike County, Missouri, too, along with Pike Moore. These three men were Indian fighters, trappers, and hunters, as well as prospectors. You take old Horn Miller...if you heard his gun, you'd know whose shot it was. He poured his own gun powder. He had a 50 calibre rifle, an old buffalo gun, it was. He was a dead shot with it and with his six shooter, too. Never caught Horn Miller without both his guns.

"Then there was Tom Newcomb and Liver-Eatin' Johnson —

both of them was scouts for General Crook when the Indians were on the warpath. Tom is well known in Park County for having killed the fastest gunman we had in the West, California Joe. One day Tom was ridin' into Crook's camp with dispatches. He had an antelope on his saddle he had killed a ways back on the trail. Johnson was the first one he met in camp and he said to Tom, 'Do you care if I eat some of your antelope? The Indians have scared all the game out of the country. I haven't had fresh meat for a week.'

" 'Help yourself,' says Tom, who had ridden a long way and was ready to turn in. Tom said he saw Johnson with a fire going and a kettle on the fire when he went to bed and thought that the next morning he would have some of the antelope for breakfast. In the morning Tom found Johnson by his dying campfire, sound asleep, and a pile of bones beside him. He had eaten the whole antelope."

Horn Miller knew Johnson well; they rode side by side when both of them were scouts for General Nelson A. Miles. Horn was one of the few frontiersmen left alive at the turn of the century. After fifty years as a mountain man, he settled in with the Randalls. He was known to be a man who told the truth, so his account of Liver-Eating Johnson is probably nearer the fact than most stories that have grown up over the years.

"Horn vowed that Liver Eater was the most surly man he ever knew....The Indians called him Black Bear. He was feared and sought after by the Sioux and Blackfeet tribes, probably more than any other man. He is credited with killing more Indians for their scalps than any other white man. He was a man of tremendous strength, standing six-and-one-half feet high, weighing some 250 pounds without an ounce of fat on his huge frame. He had more endurance and stamina than any other man in the Territory....His large head was covered with shaggy long hair, which he occasionally trimmed, together with his stained whiskers, with his razor-sharp hunting knife."*

Another pioneer told the Randalls that John Johnson had been

---

* Randall, Gay, FOOTPRINTS ALONG THE YELLOWSTONE. The Naylor Co., San Antonio, Texas, 1961. p. 116.

born in New Jersey in the summer of 1824 of English parents and was in turn a sailor, prospector, army scout, hunter, wolfer, whiskey smuggler and wood cutter.

It was at the mouth of the Musselshell River, according to Gay Randall's book, that Johnson got his famous name. "Captain Hawley kept a trading post there....On a day in July, Mrs. Hawley and a friendly squaw ventured some distance from the post to pick berries. Suddenly they were fired upon by a raiding party of Sioux warriors."* Mrs. Hawley was shot through the neck and appeared dead. The Indian woman ran for help and one of the men who responded was Johnson. They found that Mrs. Hawley was alive but had been scalped by the Indians. They carried her back to the Post and she lived for many years, always wearing a wig.

A battle ensued between the Indians and the wolfers with the final outcome being 30 Indians dead. "Johnson opened up the belly of one of the dead warriors and took out the liver. Holding it high in the air, he said, 'Who will have their liver rare?' Several men came up to Johnson, pretending, but backed away sickened by the sight, when they saw that he was carving off slices of the still warm Indian liver and eating it raw."

The Liver Eater, as Horn Miller called him, liked to demonstrate his physical strength and his expertness with a rifle. Like all mountain men, he lived off the land and he took pride in killing animals with his bare hands.

Sometime in the late 1850's, Johnson decided it was time he got a wife, so he gathered his horses, the winter's catch of furs, and some extra guns and headed for the Flathead country. There he traded some of these things to Chief Bear's Head in return for a pretty teen-age daughter.

"When fall came, Johnson's trapping partner, Del Gue, came to Johnson's cabin on the Little Snake and they made preparations for the winter's trapping expedition....Johnson had become very fond of his squaw who was now with child, and he hesitated to leave her alone, but a man had to earn his livelihood....When the first snow

*Op. cit. p. 119.

18

came he left....Swan was well provided for and comfortable in the log cabin....It was a long hard winter for Johnson. He trapped harder than ever before, planning on the fine things he would buy for his child from the traders come spring, when he sold his furs....When they arrived back at the cabin, they found Swan had been killed and the cabin ransacked.*

"For the next ten years, Johnson relentlessly sought out the Indians responsible for Swan's death and killed many others in avenging it. He once again became the most feared man in the Territory."

Dick Randall's first hand knowledge of these characters from the Old West and his association with men like Horn Miller gave color and excitement to the stories he was later to tell around camp fires. Eastern dudes and foreign dignitaries alike thrilled to Dick's stories.

---

* Op cit. p. 122 (Authenticated biography of Johnson is in this book. pages 115 to 129)

HIDEOUT TO HAVEN

Dick and Dora Randall worked long hours to get their place in order when they first moved to the ranch. He built a kitchen and a couple of bedrooms onto the little cabin the outlaws had used. He built corrals, a blacksmith shop, a barn and a good sized root cellar. They cleared the sage brush and plowed an area for Mrs. Randall's garden.

In winter, Dick went to the timber and got wood to be dried and split into stove-wood lengths. In winter, too, he guided hunters, his only means of getting cash. Dick liked guiding; he loved the mountains and the associations with people from the outside world. During the time in Yellowstone, he had broadened his acquaintances and many of his stage passengers were coming back for "another ride with Dick." It wasn't long before he had to put up tents for hunters because they couldn't all get in the log house. Some wanted to make arrangements for their sons to spend the summer with the Randalls. Eventually whole families came and little by little the dude ranch business was developing.

The Randall family now numbered four; Helen Elizabeth was born on June 30, 1898 in the little log house that straddled the line between Montana and Yellowstone Park.

Occasionally, Dick would take his family down to Chico Hot Springs for a week's vacation, and here they would get acquainted with more people interested in hunting trips.

Chico was about 25 miles from the ranch, but on the other side of the Yellowstone River. There was only one road, a narrow trail that ran between Gardiner and Livingston. There was one bridge across the river at Gardiner and another one at Emigrant. The only way to travel then was with a team of horses and a two-seated surrey,

Mt. Lockhart is snow covered the year round and only a few hours horseback ride from the ranch.

Everybody's friend, Dick Randall, genial host and owner of the OTO.

Pictured here are Mr. and Mrs. Charles Ritchie from Chicago and Mr. and Mrs. Walter Caldwell.

There wasn't much of a station at Corwin Springs, but incoming dudes were apt to be met by a bevy of mounted guests as well as the ranch hosts.

Trail riders liked to pause on this hillside to enjoy a panoramic view of the Yellowstone River. "Watchit, though," warns the guide "because just over the next hill was where Bess got into the rattlesnake den."

Some of the first dudes at the OTO on a Yellowstone Park trip. Robert Schram from Chicago is on the left. Next to him is Catherine Simon whose article about this dude ranch was published in the Literary Digest. *Helen Nearing from Pennsylvania, Mr. Jennings, manufacturer and his two sons complete the party.*

Chuck wagon dinners added atmosphere.

Dick took Charlie Herbert, then an unknown and broke photographer, into the high country on a photo safari. The pictures they got of wild animals were bought by Pathe News and started Herbert on a successful career.

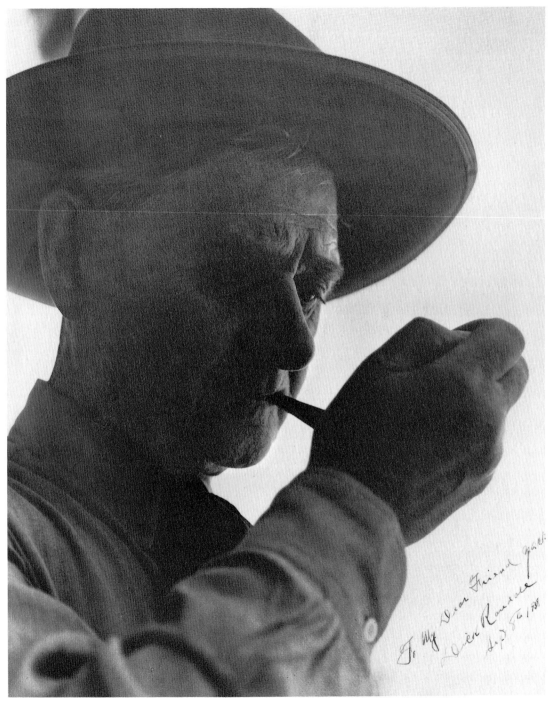

Lighting up. Dick was seldom seen without his pipe.

Mother Randall, genteel, genial and efficient hostess and manager at the OTO.

Dudes and guides on an all day ride to the head of Cedar Creek.

Wrangler Bill Randall showing Kay Brown
of New York City how to hold a lariat rope. —UM

"Where's my breakfast?" (Bill and George Randall)

Dudes gather at the corral waiting for wranglers to bring their horses.
Dick Randall, top left was always on hand to see that everything was in order.

Fresh trout for breakfast.

Part of the 368 member Sierra Club trip around Yellowstone Park. People walked but it took 80 pack horses and 16 packers to handle the luggage, food, cook stoves & tents.

Bill Randall learned from his grandfather what to pack for camp cooking. —UM

Fly casting lesson. Dick Randall and a dude. —Museum of the Rockies

The big OTO lodge was finished in 1930.

The OTO lodge was decorated with trophies of the hunt.

The famous "Buckaroo" designed and built by Clyde Erskine and Charlie Herbert, later owner of Western Ways Photo Shop in Tucson. The "buckaroo" was featured in an eastern newspaper account of the ranch. —Museum of the Rockies

This five room cabin is complete with bath. Dick Randall couldn't believe guests would be willing to pay extra for such frills as indoor plumbing.

Angora chaps were high fashion at the OTO.

All the bucking horses and trick riders weren't in the rodeos!

so the family had to travel 50 miles around by Gardiner to get to Chico; or they could ford the river and save 25 miles. Sometimes in late fall bottom ice would jam the river by breaking into big blocks. This was called anchor ice and when it broke away, it would float down the river. If the Randalls had to cross when ice chunks were floating, Dick would give the reins to Dora and get down onto the step of the surrey and push the chunks of ice out of the way so they could get through without upsetting. This was dangerous and took a lot of nerve, but Dick and his family had that kind of pioneer courage.

While at Chico, Dick would swim in the pool to soothe his aching muscles and then take treatments from Dr. Corwin. The treatments were helpful, but a business venture that developed with the doctor was a fiasco for Dick.

One day, Dr. Corwin said, "I wish I could find a hot springs like they have here." Dick said he knew of one and the two men struck up a deal and made plans for future development. Dick wanted a place where he could bring his guests, and the doctor envisioned a Health Spa, patterned after those in Europe.

Later, Dick took two men to the spot he had picked and they managed to elevate the hot water about nine feet above the edge of the Yellowstone River. It was an ideal place for a swimming pool, with natural hot water and a good place for buildings. This was a short distance down-river from Chico Hot Springs. Dr. Corwin began planning for an elaborate hotel; Dick wanted a place where his guests could eat and sleep while he handled hunting parties, the stages and surreys. They acquired ten acres so there would be good pasture for horses. Dr. Corwin insisted they call the place "Corwin Springs." The big hotel was built and the men formed a corporation and sold stock in the new venture. Each man put in $20,000 and Dick went to Butte to sell stock in the corporation. While there, he bought Dora a beautiful silk dress, paid $100 for it, and made great plans that she would wear it for the opening of the resort.

They got a few business men interested in investing. The corporation elected officers: Dr. Corwin, president; Dick, secretary-treasurer. John Sharp went to Chicago and bought expensive furnishings for the hotel. He had not been authorized to do it, but he did. Corwin was not running the project as Dick felt it should be run and he knew he was gradually being squeezed out, so he said, "Gentlemen, my stock is for sale. If you don't want to buy it, I will put it on the open market tomorrow."

It was Dick Randall's first big dream and it had fallen through. He wanted his guests to have the best, but he could see this arrangement would never work, so he disposed of the Corwin property and went back to his place on Cedar Creek. From that time on, Dick stuck to the OTO and the dudes he loved. Mother Randall never wore the beautiful silk dress except for one family portrait.

Dick Randall was determined to have a place of his own where he could accommodate guests and then take them out on hunting trips. Guiding was the most profitable thing he could do, so he leased land from the Forest Service at Hell Roaring Creek about 22 miles from Gardiner. This was a vast, rugged area few people had ever explored. Fishing was great and the country abounded with deer, elk, moose, bear, and mountain sheep. Here at Hell Roaring, Dick built a hunting lodge. Everything except fire-wood had to be brought in by pack horses.

Randall had two horses he could pack anything on and know they would deliver the load safely at camp. Dandy always carried the eggs, which had been packed in sawdust for the trip. After Dick had Dandy's packs filled and the diamond hitch thrown to hold all in place, he headed the horse toward the camp trail, turned him loose and knew full well the pack horse, with eggs unbroken, would be at the hunting Lodge before he could get there. Sometimes when Dandy was in a pack string, he would leave the group because he couldn't get through the regular trail with the bulky packs he had. He would pick his way through the forest, finding open areas, and he invariably arrived at the hunting lodge the same time the other horses did.

The other pack horse was Buck, a tall, slender buckskin who carried a cookstove and sometimes lumber into Hell Roaring Camp.

During construction of the camp, Buck could often be seen coming along a mountain trail with lumber sticking out over his rump. He, too, would pick his own trail. On the way to Hell Roaring, the horses had to go down a very steep grade and then up over Specimen Divide. Buck, with his load of lumber could not follow such a steep trail down because the weight of the lumber would lift his back feet right off the ground. So the wise old pack horse would twist around and shift the weight so he could get all four feet on the ground and then zig-zag down the hill to keep his load balanced. Dick could always count on Buck arriving safely at camp with his load of lumber.

Now, with extra cabins at the OTO home place and the camp in the mountains, Dick could take care of hunters and their families. Montana's first dude ranch was a reality.

"Here we have the greatest outdoor country in the world," Randall wrote in his Memoirs, "with our lakes and streams and mountains. There was always wild game, and streams full of fish, but they let the damn sheep get in and drive them out. As soon as the sheep silt gets carried to our water, fish are no longer gamy fish at all. The sheep herders make their camps and bed down the sheep right on the streams."

In later years, Randall ran cattle but he could never tolerate what bands of sheep did to mountain pastures, and he felt the indiscriminate homesteading was a tragedy for the people as well as the land.

"The National Forests shouldn't have been handled the way they were. We permitted dry-land farming in eastern Montana and that was the beginning of it. We went to work and ruined one of the best cow countries that ever was — bunch grass, blue joint and blue grass. Dry-land farmers brought in families and they starved out trying to make a living on 160 acres. Sheep men and cattle men got along for awhile because sheep men could use the high ranges that cattle couldn't get to. When the National Forest was created, they began to move sheep into the foothills. They found water from mountain streams was good for the sheep. It was the feed growing in mountain country that made plenty of milk for lambs.

"But that was the same feed that had brought our wild game through the winter. The sheep went up into these forests and they stripped out all the underbrush. We never had forest fires long ago. The underbrush held snow and moisture. Now we have a big run off when the sun hits in June. It used to be damp clear through August. Now, with the underbrush gone the sun hits in June, and the snow melts too fast and water runs along the side of the mountain bringing silt into our mountain lakes and streams. That silt kills fish.

"There were 35 to 40,000 head of elk when I first started hunting; now there's not more than 7,000 elk and maybe 2,000 deer. There's no feed to pull a big herd through the winter."

Dick Randall was aware of the devastation resulting from overgrazing; he knew most homesteading was a tragic mistake but he had a great natural love of people and it was with real sadness that he saw impoverished homesteaders trying valiantly to eke out a living. One of his happiest memories was of a Christmas when he and June Buzzell were able to bring some holiday joy to a few of these families.

The following story was published first in *Dude Rancher Magazine* and then reprinted in *Montana, The Magazine Of Western History.**

A CHRISTMAS STORY FROM THE WEST
by
Dick Randall

It was after the hard winter of 1886 that the "nesters" began to engulf Montana. The cattle barons had no use for nesters even though these homesteaders and ex-cowboys had as much right to the open ranges as the big cow outfits. They would locate near a water hole, having a piece of bottom land and a small meadow, usually several milk cows and often a large family of children.

The old time cowboy was for the nester. It was probably his family that touched the soft spot of the cowboy. There was never a Christmas went by that line riders for the big outfits wouldn't

*Reprinted here with permission from MONTANA, THE MAGAZINE OF WESTERN HISTORY. Winter 1957, pp. 28-31.

pool their wages and make up a kitty for the nesters' families.

Our nearest store was at the little cow town of Junction City, twenty-five miles away. The cowboys would ride to town for a little Christmas cheer and there was always one in the group we could trust with the bank roll and the Christmas shopping.

My partner for that winter's line-riding was a fellow by the name of June Buzzell, a good natured cowboy and a good pal to hole up with for the winter. We had three nesters' families in our circle rides. All had from two to four children. One of the boys from the home ranch brought our share of the Christmas stuff which we had already talked about .dividing among the three families.

Well, one morning I said to June, "Let's saddle up our ponies and call on our nester friends. You know tonight is Christmas Eve and let's start with Jim Neal."

Jim had the largest family, four children. When we reached Jim's place we found him in the corral, tears streaming down his face.

"What's the trouble, Jim?" we asked.

"Well, my wife's pet cow 'Flossie' had a calf last night and it was dead. I am afraid to tell her," he replied.

"How long's it been dead?" June asked.

"Not long, it's still warm."

I was doing some quick thinking. Finally I said, "June, you and Jim go and skin the calf out. Get all the skin from the legs and don't let the Mrs. know what you're doing. I am goin' to take a ride up Cow Creek. Don't let the skin get cold, no matter what.

June had a hunch about what I reckoned to do. Before I ever got to the big alkali marsh on Cow Creek I heard a calf bawling. It had a squeaky voice like it was about the tail end of its bawling. I hurried my horse, Poison, up thinking it might be a lobo wolf that had the calf.

When I came into sight of the marsh, there was an old mossy back cow bogged down to her sides in the center of that marsh and her baby bawling his head off and running around the marsh. I took down my rope and tied onto old bossy. The first cast just did make her head. But I had scared her baby who was high tailing it up the creek. It was a good thing I had another rope on my saddle. That little slick-ear gave me a hot chase until my loop settled on him.

Now I was up against it again. A rope on his mother and only one way to get the calf to his Ma — pack him on old Poison. I had never tried to go double on him. He was as good as gold on a rope. I boosted the little slick-ear into the saddle seat and I slipped in back of him. Everything went fine until Little Slick tried to move. One of his sharp toes raked old Poison down the neck. Then things happened. Trying to stay up there and still hold that old cow's baby was one ride which I will always remember. There was no rider near to holler "Stay with him," or "Powder River!"

Well, Poison finally got the steam out of his system and we circled back to Little Slick-ear's mother. Slipping off my horse, I hogtied the little rascal so that I could get his mother out of the swamp. "And here, Poison, is where I get even with you," I thought.

We have pulled cows out of swamps before but this old moss back must have been locoed to get herself in the fix she was in. "This is going to be the hardest pull you ever made and I hope we don't break the rope, it happens to be my best one," I told Poison. The first pull the rope I had left on the old cow tightened around her horns. Poison pulled her head around to her side. We pulled from every angle and finally got her on her side. Then I knew Poison would get her out.

What a sorry sight she was, plastered with alkali mud until it was hard to tell her color. Now came the hard part to clean away that mud so that the little shaver could find his "Fountain of Youth."

He done a lot of bucking until I got what-makes-big-steers into his mouth. His little tail began to wiggle. His side began to roll out. It was worth the hard work to see his happy expression.

"Now, Pardner, I'm goin' to choke you off. You're going to have another mother to milk out." I took the rope off the old mossback, knowing she would be on the prod when she got on her feet and that you usually get horns for such trouble. By this time, Poison was sure tired and willing to carry double without fuss. We soon made it back to the nester's place. It didn't take long to tie the hide from old Flossie's calf on the little live one.

The substitution worked.

Flossie liked to have run the calf down trying to tell him she was his mother. Old Jim Neal couldn't believe what he saw. He didn't let his wife come into the corral.

"Well, it's time for us to be goin'," June and I got on our horses. "See if you can find a jack pine tree for Christmas and we'll be back after supper to help trim it," we said to Jim as we left.

As we rode back to camp our talk was of such nesters trying to make a living and fighting for their rights. As we reached the cabin and tied up our horses, we were eager to open the sack the boys had brought from the home ranch. We took our list out. As June took the stuff out of the gunny sack, I checked off a pair of mitts and cap for old Jim, warm stockings and overshoes for his wife, size 5. "Now the kids — their little girl, how old would you say she is? June had his head poked in the sack.

"It isn't on the calendar and we didn't get it on our list, but I reckon she's about six."

"Well, I hope Buck got the right sizes. He knows the family well."

"Here's a dress for a 10 year old; may be a little large but she'll grow into it. A pair of mitts size 10. Overshoes, size 8. Well, I reckon that's about right for one gal. Now the boys: we'll start at 5 and drop a number for each one, four, three, two size over-shoes for boys. They can switch around until they find a pair they can wiggle into, just like cowboots. If you can get in 'em an soak 'em down, they'll fit. Now get the other sack, June, should have 5 pounds of hard candy. We'll leave half of that here to take to the other families."

Ten pounds of mixed nuts and ten more pounds of popcorn completed our gifts. We got flour sacks, divided the nuts and corn into them and were on our way like old Saint Nick himself.

As we rode along, June opened up more than usual. He talked a lot about his hard life in North Dakota. He had never opened up like this. I guess the Christmas spirit caught him off guard. His father's and mother's families both was squatters and in that hard winter of '86 they lost all their stock.

June wanted to know then about that old cow I pulled from

the alkali bog. She was a rack of bones, which meant the wolves and coyotes would be picking her bones and the little calf would have died before a week, I told him.

"Wal, in that case," drawled June, "I think it was a kind act that you did. You saved the calf and it will sure mean a lot to Jim's wife, that poor old soul. She has had so little in this world, raising four children with so little to go on. I'll be anxious to see her face when she sees that calf."

"Here we are, let's take the hide off the calf before we go to the house."

In the corral stood old Flossie licking her new calf's hide and the Little Slicker was getting his bread basket full of good warm milk.

Jim had shooed the kids off to bed and we got to work on the tree. June said he would cook the popcorn. He wanted me to fix the tree as he had never seen a Christmas tree all decorated up.

"If you've got some syrup," I said to Mrs. Neal, "we'll make some popcorn balls to hang on the tree."

"She's a poppin' fine," called June from the end of the cabin that served as a kitchen.

Mrs. Neal brought out some cotton battin' left over from making quilts and I threw little patches all through the green tree. Jim nailed the tree to a small box and I covered the box with cotton battin', too. We made popcorn balls and strung them for the tree. Jim cracked a big dish full of nuts. There was a heapin' dish of candy, too. We needed some candles, so Jim took them out of his lanterns. We lit one and used it to stick the others to the board floor around the tree. The presents were put under the tree. The boys all together, so they could have the fun an' excitement of picking out their sizes. The little girl's stuff was put separate. The candles would let Santa read the names on the packages, June said.

Finally we were all set to let the kids in. It was something I will always remember. Those little kids just stood and stared. Finally they went for the candy and popcorn balls. The little girl, Jane, picked up the dress while Mrs. Neal stood with her mouth open and tears running down her face. Jim was spellbound.

Mrs. Neal asked me to read something Jim had written on a

piece of paper. It said: "A nice bull calf in the corral getting his stomach full of Flossie's milk."

Well, she broke out of the door like a spooked antelope and ran to the corral. When she got back she rushed to Jim, threw her arms around him and gave him a big kiss.

I think June and I were both kids again that day. It took so little to make a body happy in those days. It was hard to break away from the Neals, but finally we saddled up and rode back to our camp. Ed Hinsdale and Tom Spellman were our next calls for Christmas, and I think June and I talked all night about those kids and the grateful look in Jim's eyes as he said, "Good night and God bless you, boys. I will never forget you or the little slick-ear calf which made the Mrs. so happy. We will get our brand on him soon and he won't ever know he was a little orphan."

This was the way Christmas was back in the years when the cowboy was in his prime and the cattle barons had our ranges stocked with southern cattle eatin' our precious God-given grass, but all was right with the world because there was peace on earth an' good will among men.

EUROPEAN GEOLOGISTS

"I carried the mail one winter on the run to Cooke City from Mammoth. Dave Yancy's run was to Tower Falls; mine was from Yancy's Roadway Inn to Tower Falls. Dave Seaman's run was from there to Cooke City — 20 miles, most always done on snowshoes. Specimen Mountain was on my run and I often saw 30,000 head of elk in one herd. We had to stake our road out with willows early in the fall. We would stick willows in the ground but sometimes when the snow got deep, the elk would come along and eat the willows, so we couldn't tell where the trail was. We started out using saddle horses in the fall but ended up using snowshoes before spring. The big elk herd would move from Specimen Mountain over across LeMarr onto Slough Creek and then to Hell Roaring. Sometimes a bad storm would hit them and there'd be a loss, but not like we have today. Then, there was more feed. The average life of an elk is eight years; some of the old fellows are bound to winter kill."

Yellowstone Park was opening up. Congress had set it aside as a National Park and the army had come in to establish a post. Geologists from all over the world were coming to Yellowstone to study its unusual formations. Dick Randall was knowledgeable about the area and he owned a string of horses, so his services were much in demand.

"Arnold Haig did some of the first geological work in the Park. He issued an invitation to foreign countries to send their geologists over, and twenty-seven of them came. Some of them couldn't speak U.S. very good and that made it interesting. The geologists had a mule outfit and I furnished the saddle horses. We got lined up at Mammoth. I had one big white horse called Soldier — bought him from the government after he had killed an officer and been condemned by the Army.

"There was this one Englishman in the party and nothing would do but he wanted to ride Soldier. I told him that was a pretty tough horse, but he gave me to understand he knew a lot about horses and wanted that one. He got on Soldier and started off on a dead run. I said to him and to the others when I finally caught up, 'You fellas are going out for about 30 miles and if you don't want to ruin those horses, hang onto the bridles and slow down.' I saw the Englishman was fighting his horse all the time, kicking him and jerking him, so I worked up and figured I'd better ride along side.

"I had 27 geologists on this pack trip and every one of them had a hammer and a sack tied to the saddle horn. Every time we would come into camp, we would have about 500 pounds of rock.

"Well just as I edged up 'longside the Englishman, Soldier threw his head down and bucked him off. The geologist was humiliated because he had been so cocky about his riding. That night he went to Mr. Haig. 'Mr. 'Aig,' he says 'These 'orses are not at all like the buck jumpers we 'ave in Australia. These 'ides their heads and it's 'ard to remain in the saddle. The vicious brute would have stomped me to death if it 'adn't been for the guide.'

"For seven or eight years, June and I would go into the Park and rent out rigs and pack outfits. Then the Park Service put restrictions on it and they didn't let no outsiders come in.

"In winter we had big game hunting. The hunting started in September and ended in the latter part of November. Then we would go hunting by ourselves and pack out game for the market. We supplied mining camps with elk. We sold front quarters for three cents a pound and hind quarters for four cents. When we had sold our meat, we went back to camp and holed up like bears for the winter. The horses rustled for themselves, but we did go out and ride the range about once a week to look for them; we didn't feed any in those days.

"Bear Gulch was one mining camp we supplied; Aldrich, the coal camp, was another. Gardiner was the outfitting point, so we often sold to hotels and unloaded most of the meat for the mining camps right there. We hunted in North Cottonwood Basin, Hell Roaring Basin, and Buffalo Fork on Slough Creek. Cinnabar was an old coal town, too. It was founded by Harry Hore years before. The Conrad Company of Great Falls found that it was good coking coal. Gibson, the senator, was a member of that company; so was T.C. Powers, Dan Foweree, and Nelson Story. We kept them all in elk meat.

"We shipped a lot of meat into Livingston, too. The railroad built the National Park branch line from Livingston and they got up as far as Cinnabar, near where Gardiner sits now. The land along there was owned by Mrs. McCutcheon and she wouldn't give them any kind of rights, so the railroad stopped right there. Cinnabar was the end of the road along about 1884. A little hamlet sprung up there and travelers were sent by stage from Cinnabar into the Park. They used six-horse teams for that five-mile trip."

HUNTING GUIDE
TO DUDE RANCHER

Around the turn of the century, when lions and grizzlies were still more numerous than environmentalists, hunters were hired by the government to cut down the population of these two wild animals. Dick Randall and Buffalo Jones had a pack of hunting dogs and spent several winters tracking mountain lions. Sometimes they had twenty hunting dogs at the OTO, and a high fence was built to keep them in. The men bought blocks of cracklins from the butcher shop in Gardiner and Mother Randall made great kettles of corn meal each day to feed the dogs; Buffalo Bill Jones was the man Zane Grey wrote about in his book, *When A Man's A Man.*

Dick bought the two famous lion dogs, named Bill and Badge, that Teddy Roosevelt had taken on all his hunts. The dogs came to love Mother Randall and the children and Dick knew those two dogs would protect his family while he was in the mountains. ''There were some pretty rough neighbors in that area when we first bought the ranch.''

Randall and Jones had worked together in the mountains and decided they would go into business together. Their plan was to raise Galloway cattle and cross them with buffalo, but it was never successful.

Jones came to the ranch one day to see Dick, who was out in the meadow irrigating. Bess, then seven years old, said she would walk out to the field and tell her Dad that Jones was there. Between changes of water, Dick was breaking a colt and when Bess saw he had Cross Patches there, she asked to ride him back to the ranch. Dick hesitated because the colt was pretty frisky, but Bess coaxed and he gave in. It was hard for Dick to ever refuse Bess anything. He boosted her into the saddle and was holding the reins when her little dog, Bobbie, ran in and bit the horse's heels. The colt broke into a run with the reins flying out of reach and the little dog was right behind.

Cross Patches, heading for the barn, went under some low tree limbs and Bess was knocked off and fell to the ground unconscious. Dick rushed to her finding her lip cut so badly her teeth were sticking through. He took her to the house and pulled the cut lip together, securing it with adhesive tape. The next day he rode 17 miles to Mammoth Hot Springs for a doctor's advice. The doctor said Dick had done all he could, and that the lip should have a change of dressing every day. It healed without a scar.

Dick was especially interested in health and many times used his skills in this land and age of sparse medical facilities. He had been named for two doctors, Dr. James and Dr. Norris who were present at his birth. By the time he was ten, he was driving the buggy for these two doctors as they went about rural areas making house calls. Young Dick listened to their discussions of cases and cures, asking as many questions as he dared. The physicians became very fond of the boy and called him "Little Doc." One of Dick's real satisfactions in hosting dudes in the years to come was to improve their health. He was convinced that fresh air and good country food, along with plenty of horse-back riding, could cure most city-bred ailments.

He was also the unofficial veterinarian for all the animals on the ranch.

"We had a brand at the ranch; it was OTO and didn't mean anything in particular. Each ranch has a brand which is put on all livestock. The simpler the brand the better. This one didn't blotch and I could make it with an iron ring and a straight bar. If I was out on the range and saw one of my critters that wasn't branded, I could make out with an iron ring, a pair of pliers, my case knife and a little brush fire. My brother, Will Randall, used it too; he put it on the hips of cattle and the shoulders of horses; sometimes calling it the Red River Cart.

"I had that brand on 300 head of horses, 30 saddles and on our cattle. Whenever I got hold of a dollar, I'd put it into cattle; built up a herd that way.

"For fifteen years, I had been booked most of the time with foreigners for hunting trips. In the fall we would hunt for bear, elk, deer, moose, sheep, and antelope. If we had a successful hunt, they would recommend me to their friends. We had people from England, Scotland, India, Germany, and all of them at one time or another lived with us in our log cabin, and many came back later as guests at the ranch. Some of these foreigners invested in business here. Lord Kinley built the Albemarle Hotel in Livingston; Lord Todd built the Toddy Building in Great Falls. Villard* hunted with me, too. He was associated with the railroads.

"Then there was Alex Mitchell from Edinborough, Scotland, and his brother-in-law, Arthur Payton from Jamacia. Back home, Alex maintained a troop of cavalry at his own expense. We called him the Colonel. We liked that man; had a letter from him shortly before he was killed at Verdun. We had great hunts, Mitchell and I. Once when we were in the Jackson Hole Country, he said to me, 'I'd better wire home for a letter of credit, I only brought $30,000 with me.' I told him we could go a long way in Montana on that, most things of value in this country don't cost big money.

"We ended that year with a buffalo hunt on the Flathead Reservation. My connection there was with Joe Allard and Pablo. They had about four or five hundred head of buffalo running on the Pondera section of the Reservation. I made a deal with Pablo, paid him $500 to let us hunt buffalo just as people did in the early days, on horseback and with Indian scouts. I had a taxidermist, Tolhurst from Livingston, with me. What these foreign hunters wanted was trophy heads. They gave the meat to the Indians. Two Indian cowboys went along with us to be sure we kept and took care of any animal we killed.

"These hunting parties lasted about two months — never less

---

* Henry Villard was president of the Northern Pacific RR and drove the Golden Spike in 1883 when the line was completed.

than two months. I would take three or four hunters in a party, but I never hunted more than two men at a time. You get too tired dodging bullets. I prefer to hunt with just one man and have him do as I tell him. No man should walk behind with a cartridge in his barrel; I'd always bring the hunter alongside me. I'm fast enough so that when I see my game, I can get a cartridge in.

"In 1919 we had 52 hunters at my ranch at one time. We had a big log building, kept fires going in the two fireplaces. I'd walk in and pick up a gun, and if I found a cartridge in it, I'd say, 'Whose gun is this?' and somebody would answer 'It's mine,' after I'd said what model it was and so forth. Then I'd yell, 'What the hell do you want to do, kill somebody? Don't never bring another gun in this house with the cartridge in the barrel; some feller might pick it up just to try it, and it might go off and kill somebody. If I ever find you bringin' that gun in the house loaded again, you've had your last hunt with me!'"

What was later to be known as the OTO Dude Ranch was just naturally developing out of popular demand. The Randalls found the hunters wanted to bring their families and spend some time in the summer, too. They started having paying guests in 1912. Easterners, especially, wanted to send their sons out to a Montana ranch for the summer. Originally, they were like Mrs. Tyler who said her son was a good husky boy and she was sure he could earn his keep and the work experience would be good for him. Randall tried out a few of those but finally decided that arrangement wouldn't work. "It just plain took too much of your time to educate somebody like that. I've had fellers tell me they know about working horses, and I've seen them lay the harness on the floor and lead the horse over to it, hoping it would jump in place, I guess. I decided if I was going to take care of anyone's kids, I'd have to get paid for it.

"We were on the OTO ranch from 1898 to 1934 and during that time other Dude Ranches were springing up in Montana and Wyoming. I met Howard Eaton in the Park. He was getting wild game from Yellowstone Park to send to zoos. He was living on the edge of the Badlands then and needed some extra money. Eaton had never hunted this area and I had a hunting party going out, so I said,

"Throw your outfit in and go along with me, and I'll tell you what I know about this country. We camped on Peace Creek down in Jackson Hole. Howard also had a contract to furnish milk cows in the Park, and each spring he would go to Minnesota and buy the cows. Then in the fall when the Park closed up, I would buy the cows. That way I built up a milk herd for the OTO and it furnished butchering stock, too.

"Montana was a good place for dude ranches because we had the greatest outdoor scenery. We didn't have game laws at first, and Wyoming didn't either. You stop along any stream and have great fishing. The setting was wild, as Nature had made it, until civilization kind of moved in on it. It was that wildness that appealed to folks.

"I used to tell people, 'If, after you've spent a month on a Montana ranch, riding horseback every day, and living outdoors, you don't feel better, you don't need a doctor, you need an undertaker, and there's no hope for you.

"On our dude ranch, each guest was assigned a horse. All reservations included a horse. I'd size up each guest and choose a horse I thought would suit and then pick out a saddle; had to be sure to get the right roll, cantle, and a proper swell in the fork, so's to make for comfort. We had special saddles for little kiddies. If guests had been used to a pancake saddle, we'd educate them to a Western one."

As the OTO grew, many kinds of activities were developed to meet the varying preferences of guests, but always Dick Randall insisted that horse-back riding was the most important.

One young man named Joe, sent out "to spend a summer with Dick Randall," proved to be almost more than even Dick could handle. The story began on a regular Old West horse-thief roundup.

Sometimes, as Dick was taking hunters into the Jackson Hole country, he would pass little bands of horses. He thought this was unusual but the horses were always in a position where he couldn't read the brand. He stored the facts in his head, but didn't investigate. Those were the days when one didn't dare get too inquisitive. Randall's livelihood depended on getting hunters into the Jackson

Hole and finding game for them. He didn't want to get any gang of horse thieves mad at him because he might wake up some morning and find all his horses gone.

"Well, it finally came out that these horses I'd been seeing were stolen ones that were trailed into Jackson Hole where the brands were worked over. Then they were shipped to Salt Lake City and sold.

"The lawmen were on their trail but most didn't know the country too well, so they asked me if I'd help them locate the horse thieves' hideout. I wasn't about to get involved in that project, but I did draw 'em some maps and point out some trails into the high country.

"I knew most of the ranchers down in the Hole wouldn't squeal on the thieves because they had to live next to them and didn't want to lose all their own horses. Some had already disappeared. Finally, the lawmen did catch up to the horse thieves. They killed the two leaders, Spencer and Bennet, and arrested some others."

Then the ranchers set about to retrieve the stock they had lost. One rancher had been raising blooded horses and was anxious to get back the missing ones. He asked Dick if he would act as guide when they started riding the mountains looking for the horses. Dick said he would but he'd have to bring Joe along.

Dick was riding herd on Joe that summer. He was the son of a wealthy steel manufacturer and pretty much a problem. Dick had offered to take him over and the boy spent several summers at the OTO. Dick and the boy's father hoped that by keeping him in the mountains every summer they could keep him away from liquor. So Dick took Joe along with the ranchers looking for the stolen horses. They travelled in a group since they had no idea whether they would meet up with remaining outlaws or not. They didn't know what to expect of the residents of Jackson Hole because it was pretty much considered to be a nest of horse thieves. No one knew what members of the gang were still there or who they were. The ranchers were tense as they drove the horses past the village and down the valley. Members of the horse thief gang wore large handkerchiefs around their necks tied with a square knot, which came to be known as the "horsethief knot."

"I had to watch Joe every minute; he was unpredictable. After we got the horses out of the Hole, we headed them for Marysville, Idaho. I got busy helping the ranchers put the horses in box cars from the stock yards; some of the animals had to be shipped home. We went on to Marysville.

"Now, Marysville was a very small town, but I lost Joe and had to go looking for him. Finally, I found him sitting on the sidewalk in front of a millinery store. Five young girls were trying hats on him, and Joe had already succeeded in getting all of them 'lit up.'

"Then about two weeks later Joe and I pulled into Upper Geyser Basin and camped a mile from Old Faithful Inn. We went to bed about 8:30, but I woke up about 9:30 and found Joe was gone.

"I knew where to look for him, so I saddled my horse and rode over to the Inn. There was Joe having the time of his life, buying drinks for everyone in the bar. I asked the bartender for the bill, and paid the $156 he owed. Joe was plastered. I picked him up and threw him over the saddle on his horse and tied him on.

"That was the end of Joe. The next morning we rode back to the ranch and I packed up his things and shipped him back to Indiana."

Dick had more success with his rehabilitation project when Lee Clagett of the Chase National Bank in New York came out to the OTO. He wanted a pack trip into the high mountain country. Dick knew this would be too much or him then, since he had been very sick. He was run down, with little appetite. Dick started to help him exercise by a little horseback riding and mountain climbing each day and gradually got him strong enough to take a pack trip. Lee's appetite returned; he was especially fond of blue grouse and Dick had them cooked for him whenever possible, but he insisted that Lee eat good, healthful foods each day. By the end of the summer his mental and physical conditions were greatly improved.

"This proved to all of us that the OTO could give health and happiness to people who were too pressured with business and eastern social life, and that is what dude ranching is all about."

Some years later, when Dick was in New York, he went to the Chase National Bank and asked to see his friend, Mr. Holly who had also been a guest at the Ranch. He was president of the bank and at the moment was in a directors' meeting, but when he heard that Dick Randall was there, he stopped the meeting and invited him in. He introduced Dick to the directors and then said, "Governor, tell these boys about that time you shot the five grizzlies." So Dick Randall from Montana sat in on the Directors' meeting and entertained the New York financiers with his stories of the Old West.

Dude ranching became big business. The Eatons built up their place in Wyoming, Randall could accommodate 100 guests at the OTO, and the Millers built up the Elkhorn in Gallatin Canyon. The Diamond J and the Jumping Horse grew up on the Madison.

Colorful pamphlets distributed by the dude ranches and the railroads described the real hospitality and freshness of the West. *With its ideal location in a mountain valley all its own, a crystal clear mountain stream running by your door, with the most beautiful back country bordering right on OTO ranch property, which is within the Absaroka National Forest....more than 2,000 acres are yours to play in...countless towering peaks, beautiful lakes, waterfalls, rushing mountain streams affording excellent fishing. Here wildlife abounds in its natural habitat. Real mountain trails in an endless choice of selection for your daily rides and pack trips, lead entirely away from all human habitation...where there are no roads, towns, or automobiles....You can ride and camp for days in these beautiful mountain ranges and valleys and enjoy the thrill of being away from everything...forget business cares and the hustle of the city. It's yours, the freedom of this unspoiled world, to know, and to enjoy the tonic of this invigorating air, where natural outdoor life make for perfect health.*

The informality of life on a dude ranch appealed to wealthy people in the early 1900's. It was a welcome relief from their lives that had become dominated by social mores, political involvements, status symbols, family traditions and the social register. They came in droves.

Formality is taboo, read the brochure, *everyone goes Western; riding apparel and sport clothes are worn on all occasions.*

Dick liked to tell about Charlie, the chore "boy", a salty old timer who was listening to Mother Randall read a letter of inquiry from a prospective guest. "And what kind of clothes should I bring for evening wear?" she wrote.

"God-a-mighty," Charlie burst in, "Anybody ought ter know enough to bring a nightshirt."

Dora Randall handled all correspondence and made the reservations. She was genteel, helpful, and amazingly efficient as she went quietly about handling kitchen and dining room activities, as well as the finances of a fast-growing business enterprise.

The brochures further explained, *The town of Dude Ranch, Montana, comprises the properties of the OTO Ranch. The post office of Dude Ranch is in our own office building; your mail is delivered every day except Sunday.* The postmaster, of course, was Mrs. Randall.

There is no set schedule of activities; you do just as you please. You may ride as much as you like, alone or in small groups, or you may join some party on daily trips up into the mountains.

From the nineties on, the OTO Ranch carried on the combined activities of cattle ranching, accommodation of guests, recreational features and big game hunting. The OTO was the pioneer dude ranch in Montana, dating back to 1898 and Dick Randall's homestead. It was a real ranch, not à mountain resort, and it was this genuine Western atmosphere that attracted the dudes and kept them coming year after year. Some of them enjoyed just watching ranch activities; others participated in the actual work of branding, rounding up cattle, and bringing in saddle horses each morning.

While we offer an extensive and varied program of entertainment, horseback riding will always be the mainspring of our sports program. You are assigned your own horse and saddle as soon as you arrive and we try to fix you up with just the horse that suits you best. The brochures were widely distributed by the railroads, who were finding this led to a lucrative passenger list.

We raise our own horses and we have spirited ones for experienced riders and gentle, well-trained ones for children and beginning riders. Our cowboy guides are fine, clean cut, honest, dependable, experienced, and will add much to your enjoyment.

The young ladies from the East found that statement alarmingly and romantically true. Alarming to parents and dude ranch operators, exciting and romantic to debutants who were chafing at the restrictions of formal social affairs and glittering, expensive, but stilted balls. Many of them actually did marry the dude ranch cowboys and settle down to become ranch wives in Montana and Wyoming.

Pictures of the individual log cabins and the main lodge, along with mountain camps and herds of horses, illustrated the brochures. *Your rendezvous will be the main lodge with its large fireplaces, living room, dining room and recreation room — all built of native logs in rustic architecture. The walls are covered with trophies of the hunt and relics and curios of the Golden Days of the West. All cabins have electric lights and running water, some with bath.*

From 4 to 6 o'clock each spring and summer morning, Mother Randall worked in her garden. Often early-rising dudes came out to help her.

The OTO has long enjoyed the reputation of serving excellent meals, the menus are as varied and enticing as we can possibly make them; the quality of the food is the best, enhanced by an abundance of vegetables from our own garden, chickens, and fresh eggs. There is plenty of rich thick cream, fresh butter, milk and buttermilk from our own dairy heard of registered, tested Guernsey cows.

The weather is generally delightful at an elevation of 5,000 feet above sea level. The days are never hot — just comfortable, and the nights are cool. There are practically no mosquitos, flies or poisonous reptiles.

There were, however, rattlesnakes in some of the remote pastures and Dick was quick to warn any guests who might be inclined to ride off by themseleves about where the rattlers were and how to watch out for them. "Now one time, my daughter, Bess," he might say, "was riding over on Slip and Slide Mountain. Harriet Taylor, a dude from St. Louis, was with her. They heard the train coming down the canyon along the Yellowstone River, so they went over to where they could see the train wind its way through the pictur-esque Canyon. Harriet road back to the ranch but Bess went on to round up some horses that separated from the bunch. All of a sudden, Bess heard a rattler; she got off her horse to pick up a rock to throw at it. Then she heard more rattlers and realized she was right in the middle of a snake mess. Now, rattlers usually won't attack unless they are distrubed, so Bess backed out just as slow and easy as she could and escaped without a bite. There's a smell to rattlesnakes, though, and you get a bunch of them together and it's bad. The odor of that nest almost got the best of Bess that time. Just don't ride past that pasture fence and you'll not get into rattler territory."

The national parks were becoming popular tourist attractions and the dude ranches in Montana featured them as an added incen-tive for summers in the West. *Our close proximity to three famous national parks, Yellowstone, Teton, and Glacier makes trips from the ranch possible. We will be glad to make arrangements for your accommodations and transportation to these parks directly from the ranch.*

We are just four-and-a-half miles from Corwin Springs, where we will meet all in-coming guests by appointment. We are twelve miles from Gardiner, the northern entrance to Yellowstone Park. The luxurious Northern Pacific trains make your trip surprisingly attractive over a scenic and very interesting route. The railway sta-tion for the Northern Pacific is at Corwin Springs, Montana. Later a siding called "Randall Station" was used for OTO guests.

At the time the brochure from which the above statements were taken was printed, the OTO could accommodate 40 guests and the rates were $45 to $60 per week. Another decade saw the OTO hosting 100 dudes at a time and the rates had gone up.

BESS WINS HER SPURS

The Randall's two children were born at the ranch and grew up with the dude business. Gay helped his father with the hunting trips. Helen Elizabeth, more often called Bess, helped her mother when necessary but she was definitely an outdoors girl and her father's pal. She loved horses as much as he did; she rode the trails, knew the mountains and the habits of game. She could lead a pack train and not get lost.

One time Dick, and Bess, acting as his off-side packer, had gone into Gardiner for supplies for the Hell Roaring Camp. When they arrived in town, officials at the Yellowstone Park station said they had been trying to contact Dick. Jerry Fenton, a photographer from England, had been sent over to get photos of wild game in Yellowstone for the English government and Dick was the only guide then able to help him. Dick said he couldn't do it for four or five days because he had to get supplies back to the camp. When the men insisted that a lot depended on Dick's guiding the photographer, Bess said, "Daddy, I can take the pack string and supplies back to camp."

"No, I couldn't let you do that, Bess. You might get in a jam handling all those pack horses by yourself. That's a tough trail into Hell Roaring."

"Then we'll get Adeline Scott to go with me. She's a good rider, and I know the two of us can do it."

So Dick packed up the horses, tightened the cinches to insure the packs would stay in place and saw the girls off with a warning not to let any horse lie down or they'd really be in trouble. The two fifteen-year-olds lined up the twelve-horse pack-string and headed for the high country. Bess rode in front to lead the string and Adeline rode behind so she could watch for any trouble with an animal or pack. Their route was 25 miles of mountain trail, through heavy timber, along narrow paths of shale on the hillside, and over the Continental Divide.

The girls, with the pack-string intact, arrived at Hell Roaring Camp late in the afternoon. Gay helped them unpack and hobbled all the horses except Adeline's. Hers never had been hobbled, so they decided it would stay with the others.

Bess gave her mother the mail and they all ate supper. After eating and reading the mail, the girls went to check the horses and found every one of them gone. Adeline's horse had started for home and all the others had followed in spite of their hobbles. Even with hobbles on, a horse can travel by sort of hopping along, and one leader was enough to get them headed for home.

Bess, Gay, and Adeline started hiking up the long, winding and steep trail after the horses. It was an eight mile hike to the top of the Divide where they caught up with the horses. They managed to surround all fourteen horses and head them back toward camp. It was too dark to try to take the hobbles off the horses; besides it was easier to control them when they couldn't go so fast. The horses ended up with sore fetlocks but the three teen-agers got back to camp soon after midnight with all the string. As they came along the switchback trail, they could look out over the valley. In the meadow near camp, they saw a light moving around and heard the toot of a bugle. When they got into camp, here came Mother Randall with an old fashioned lamp in one hand and Gay's bugle in the other. What struck the kids as funny was that Mother had never been able to get a toot out of that bugle before and she never could again, but that night she knew the noise would keep the grizzlies away, and it could be a directional signal for three youngsters picking their way down a dangerous mountain trail in the dark. Mother Randall was afraid that a grizzly had gotten the young people because they were afoot and had been gone so long. That was the only time she ever got upset or afraid while camping at Hell Roaring.

Years before, when Bess was only twelve, she and her dog

Bobbie were roaming around the mountain tops above Hell Roaring Creek. Bess was on her horse, Calamity Jane, with the dog always right at her heels. On this particular day, Bobbie ran up the trail ahead of Bess and jumped a big timber wolf. Bess always carried a 22 revolver which she used to kill grouse. Now, she took one look at the timber wolf coming down the trail toward her, pulled out her gun and shot it three times. The wolf bolted for Horse Creek and swam across. Bess had to cross on a fallen tree and she could see that the wounded wolf was hemmed in by a sheer wall. He turned on Bobbie, but the dog was too fast for the wolf. He had been trained to hunt bear and now he kept himself between Bess and the wolf. When the wolf started toward her again, Bess shot at him several times. Finally, she realized she had only one shell left in her gun. Her father had always told her to save the last shot for an emergency, and since Bess didn't think this was an emergency, she finished killing the wolf with a club. Bess tried hard to hoist the wolf onto her saddle horse, but it was too heavy for a twelve-year-old to lift. She sat on a nearby log for awhile to be sure the animal was dead and then went back to camp to get help to bring the wolf in.

She was a sight; her long hair was down, her clothes in shreds and she had scratches on her face and hands from going through the brush.

When Bess arrived back in camp, her father had just come in with two hunters from Joplin, Missouri. He was delighted with the skill and resourcefulness of his daughter. The two hunters shook their heads in disbelief, and months later, after they had returned to Missouri, a package came in the mail for Bess. It was a pair of beautifully mounted silver spurs with her name engraved on each.

Dick and Gay stayed in camp or at the OTO during the fall hunting season. About Christmas time they joined Mother and Bess in Florida; Bess was then going to school in Florida. Dick felt it was very important for members of his family to mingle with people from other parts of the country and he insisted his children have good educations.

Bess graduated from Iowa State College and was a member of Pi

Beta Phi sorority. The little girl who had killed a timber wolf at twelve and led a pack train throught the mountains was equally at home on a college campus and in sorority society. Like her father, Bess loved people and charmed them wherever she went. She was an accomplished and natural musician, and in later years her music was to be the center of dude ranch evening entertainment.

Mother Randall knew a little about music and taught Bess to finger tunes on the old-fashioned pump organ. When she was five years old, she could hear a piece and then go home and play it.

One summer, Dick took two ladies from Doylestown, Pennsylvania on a pack trip, and then on a guided tour through Yellowstone Park. After they had gone home, he got a wire from one of them, Elizabeth Lawrence, asking him to go to Gardiner to pick up a package they were sending to Bess. Dick saddled his horse and rode the twelve miles to Gardiner. The "package" turned out to be a piano, carefully crated and shipped by train from Pennsylvania.

Dick rode back to the ranch, hitched a four-horse team to a dead-axe wagon and went back to the train station. He hauled that piano home to the ranch over steep mountain roads, even fording the Yellowstone River with it in the wagon. The beautiful *Ludwig* piano arrived, still in perfect tune. That was the beginning of Bess's musical career and her entertainment of dudes from all over the world. This fine musical instrument, now almost three-quarters of a century old, is in the Livingston ranch house, still in perfect tune, and its rich mahogany finish restored. One summer the Randalls bought Navajo rugs to decorate the walls and put on the floor of the OTO Lodge. Dick thought the piano should match, so he got a can of paint and painted it bright red.

Bess majored in Home Economics at Iowa State. Her mother was a wonderful cook and at one time also worked as a professional seamstress; she taught Bess to cook and sew. Her father had taught her bits of nature lore, how to run a ranch and how to hunt. She seemed as adept at one as the other.

Perhaps she told the Pi Phis about the time she had gotten off her horse to pick wild strawberries and when she stood up, she was face to face with a grizzly bear. Bess realized she was in his territory and that he had planned on those strawberries for lunch, so she ran for her horse and "got the hell out of there quick." Or she might have just played Beethoven for rush parties and waited until she got back to the ranch each summer to enjoy her wilderness and her mountains.

It was at Iowa State that Bess met Clyde Erskine and from that time on, Clyde became an important part of the OTO Ranch and its activities.

Clyde finished his hitch with the U.S. Marines in 1919, went back to his home in Iowa for a brief stay, then headed for Montana. He tells how Dick Randall breaks in a son-in-law:

> I decided to go to Montana to see Bess, the girl I was engaged to, and to meet her parents. I found them to be loveable people. Dick was knowledgeable and capable. He was also a fine entertainer and I, too, soon fell under the spell of his stories and recognized his ability to handle people. Mrs. Randall was petite and wiry, an educated and efficient person. Her formal schooling had been limited but she was widely read and on her own studied law, psychology and medical books. Her endurance and her wonderful disposition were an inspiration to all of us.
>
> Bess was happiest when helping her Dad with the cattle or horses. Her brother and his wife lived at the OTO and had a young family coming on.
>
> In April of 1920, I returned to the OTO; we planned to be married in June, but the big Lodge wasn't finished and Bess wanted to be married in it, so the wedding was put off until September. I'm sure Dick also wanted to find out if there was any work to be gotten out of his future son-in-law. He might have been a bit jealous too because Bess was very dear to him.
>
> When I first arrived at the ranch that spring, I was a little green on Western ways and the Governor really put me through the paces. He had a pet horse he called Silvertip. She was the best of the pack-string and as the lead horse always wore the bell. Well, this bell-mare got the colic very bad. The Governor, who

was a good horse doctor along with his other skills, asked me to help him treat the horse. First we poured a quart of good old Grandad whiskey down her. This whiskey belonged to a friend of Dicks, but it did no good for Silvertip. He showed me how to inject soap into her rectum. So I peeled off my shirt and put soap in my hand and inserted it as far as I could reach. I kept at it all morning, but the horse died, and I was mightily embarrassed about it all. I guess the Governor decided I'd make a good hand on the ranch even though he lost his favorite horse and also the friend that had owned the bottle of Grandad. But I got Bess!

Dick had our wedding all planned; he wanted us all on horseback. He had several western saddle ponies that would march in time to music, and even the minister, he planned, would be on a horse.

Bess said no; she wanted a regular wedding with a veil, white gloves, and me in a tuxedo. Bess had recently graduated from Iowa State and had taken an active part in campus social activities. She had ideas of her own. Much as she loved this far corner of the West, where she had been raised and would spend most of the rest of her life, she wanted a traditional wedding with all the niceties she had observed during her years in the Midwest. The wedding was to be at the OTO Ranch and that meant, of course, that family members would make the preparations. No one had ever heard of a wedding consultant, or a flower shop in Gardiner, or a caterer to bring in food.

Bess wanted an arch of pine boughs under which we could stand during the ceremony. There had to be a platform for us and the minister, too, and two pillows for kneeling.

At 4 a.m. on the morning of the wedding, I started building that arch. Two of the dudines had gone to the mountains and gathered pine boughs for me. It took me until five o'clock in the afternoon to get that platform and arch ready. I was exhausted and heading for my room, but as I went by the kitchen door, Mother Randall called out to say that she didn't have anyone to freeze the ice-cream. It took me an hour of turning and packing ice to get that gallon-and-a-half frozen.

But one won't be enough,' Mother Randall said, 'I have the

custard made for another freezer.' So, tired as I was, I started in again, turning the handle for another hour to make the ice-cream for our wedding supper.

It was seven o'clock when I got all the chores done and went to my room to get dressed, but I fell asleep instead. At 20 minutes to eight, Bess's brother, who was to be my best man, came in and helped me scramble into my tuxedo. The wedding march was being played as we came into the Lodge.

The guests and dudes stayed for the wedding dance and supper in the big lodge recreation room, but I fell asleep standing up and Mother Randall said, 'Clyde, you'd better go to bed. I'll send Bess in when all the guests have gone.' So I did.

Bess and I were married on September 1, 1920. The next morning I asked her what she thought I should call her father. I can't call him Father, or Dad, or even Dick. What's your suggestion? Bess said that down South, children often called their father 'The Governor.' So it was 'the Governor' from then on. The dudes picked it up and they all spoke of him as the Governor. He loved it. Mrs. Randall was Mother Randall to all of us — family, cowboys, and guests.

The Governor was always last to bed; often it would be 2 a.m. "You've got to see that all the dudes are in bed," he would say to me, "and check all around, look everyplace inside the Lodge and around the other buildings to be sure no one has left a burning cigarette that could start a fire." He was very careful of fire and protective of the home ranch, as he was of the forests when he was on camping trips.

"You've got to watch the dudes when you are out with them," the Governor said to me, "see that their horses are properly saddled and the cinches are tight. Keep a sharp eye out so nothing will happen. You've even got to watch that a new dude don't try to get on the wrong side of a horse. Most of our critters will buck at that. We sure don't want anybody to get hurt." And in all our years of handling dudes, there was never a horseback accident. Occasionally a dude got bucked off, but no one was ever hurt.

One time the Governor was putting shoes on a young colt he

was breaking and a guest, Joseph Braun, an influential lumberman from Michigan, was watching him. When Dick finished with the shoes, Braun said, 'I want to ride that colt.' The Governor told him that it was only green broke and he didn't like to put anyone on a horse unless he was sure it was safe. Braun laughed at Dick's caution and said he had a stable of fourteen horses back in Detroit and felt he could ride anything the Governor could. So Dick led the horse out of the barn and told Braun to get on if he wanted to. Braun started to mount and throw his right leg over, but the colt jumped and Braun landed behind the saddle. On the next bounce, he landed in a manure pile. Of course, he was embarrassed and very dirty. He headed for his cabin, got cleaned up, and for the rest of his stay at the ranch was content to ride Laddi-Go, the horse that had been assigned to him.

FIRST FALL OF THE HINDENBURG LINE

One of Dick Randall's favorite stories was about the time he took Von Hindenburg hunting. He called it the "First Fall of the Hindenburg Line" and we will quote it here just as he wrote it for the Livingston paper:

It was in 1894, September 2, that I got a message to come to Mammoth Hot Springs in the Park to meet a hunting party. My business was guiding big game hunters, both American and foreign. Most of the foreigners were titled. Our country — Montana, Wyoming, and Idaho — was a paradise for big game hunters. There weren't any game laws and wild animals were plentiful. The man who wanted to see me identified himself as General Von Hindenburg.

"Mr. Randall," he said, "did you take Carl Von Sagivigency on a hunt?"

"Yes, and I've hunted quite a few other Germans," I answered.

"Well," said Von Hindenburg, "I'm going to cable my folks that I am putting myself in your care for 30 days in the wilds of America, and you are responsible for my safe return to civilization."

"Now, wait a minute, General, you just tell them that I will return you safe, barring an accident, and if you are dead, I'll promise to ship home your remains."

"Mr. Randall," he said, "America is very cold and unfriendly. I am going to San Francisco and will return in ten days. Then we will be ready to start."

I says, "General, I won't be able to take you at that time

because I am booked for the fall with one of my old hunters and his wife, Mr. and Mrs. James Libby Watson of Rochester, New York."

I told Von Hindenburg that my partner, June Buzzell was as good a hunter as I was and would get him the trophies he wanted. I promised to see them safely into the hunting country as my party wasn't due until the first of October.

June and I had about the biggest lot of hunting equipment in our part of the West, running over 100 head of saddle and pack horses. We were both kept busy with bear hunts in the spring and big game hunts in the fall, along with fishing and mountain climbing in the summer.

I was darn glad to sluff this trip off on June. I had found out that German officers were really hard to handle. They wanted to kill everything that got up in front of them whether it had a trophy head or not. If there were two, three, or four in the party, they wanted the guide to 'hunt' them all at once.

By the time we got the pack-string lined out, the boys had dubbed Von Hindenburg "Dutchy," and that was what he was called during the whole trip. There was June Buzzell, the guide, Billy North, the cook, and Wes Ritchie, the packer. Dutchy had arrived with an outfit that would have done for a two-year safari in Africa. Some outfitter had really seen him coming. I kept trying to sort out his stuff, putting aside things he wouldn't need. He protested every piece, and even with all the discards, we had to take two extra pack horses just to take his luggage.

"Mr. Randall," he said as we were packing, "you will take camp chairs and when we get into good hunting country, Mr. Buzzell can place the chairs for me in a good spot. Then he can drive the game to me for a good shot."

"General," I said, "We have included chairs but you will not need them for hunting in this country like you do in Germany where you have gillies to beat the brush and drive the game around to you. This hunting will really be hunting and much of it is done on foot."

"That will ruin my boots," Von Hindenburg was looking sort of disturbed. "Mr. North, the cook, will blacken my boots at night, won't he?"

"Now, General," I says, "I wouldn't ask him if I was you. These Western fellers are a little fussy, and we don't black boots in the mountains. We grease them with tallow. Now, if you see Mr. North greasin' his boots some evening, you ask him to grease yours, and I know he will."

After trying to put the General right about camp ways, we packed the horses. We put between 160 and 175 pounds on each. That was about all a horse could carry for eight hours of mountain travel, and we aimed this outfit would do about 25 miles a day. There was some cussin' when we went to load Dutchy's things on the packs. He had two long man-lickers (gun cases) with two guns in each. The saddle packs had to be built up so the horses head could work under the long cases. Many of the gadgets he had were impossible to throw a diamond hitch over. There was the acetlene lighting plant for one and a gramaphone with a big horn for another. A guide is supposed to be able to put most anything on a horse, and if it gets broken, it's the guide's fault.

We finally got under way; there were no well-defined trails. It was hard going in places, with burnt timber, fallen logs and brush from pine trees. Trying to get all that bulk along those narrow trails and through thick timber was a problem. Dutchy's useless luggage took a beating. The gramaphone horn was put out of commission and pounded up so badly no noise could come through it.

Our first camp was on Two Ocean Pass. It's called that because water from that mountain top divides and flows two ways; part of it goes into the Pacific and part of it to the Atlantic.

Dutchy got lost once while I was still with them. In every aspen thicket along the way, there were little drummer partridges we called fool hens. They really do fool you with their jerking heads and make a hard mark for a 22. Now, pack trains have to keep moving from the time packs are put on until the day's drive is over. You get in real trouble if you ever let a pack horse stop. Invariably, Dutchy would get off his horse in these aspen groves and waste a lot of time trying to shoot a fool hen. When he mounted his horse to catch up, he most always took the wrong trail and got lost. The first time it happened, it was dark before I found him, and by the time I got him back to camp, he was pretty mad. He said to the cook, "I don't like these secret camps of Mr. Randall's." He was always talking about the secret camps we put in places where he couldn't find them.

Well, before I left camp, June had helped him get a big black bear. "How did Dutchy behave?" I asked June when they came in with the bear.

"The first shot that hit the bear made him let out a bawl and that gave Dutchy buck fever, but from then on it sounded like the Battle of Gettysburg," June told me when we got off by ourselves in camp, "I was carrying Dutchy's guns and he kept those two big man-lickers hot. By the time the smoke cleared away, Dutchy was over his buck fever."

Lots of big-game hunters get buck fever, especially if it's a bear they're up against. Dutchy was happy; he had a good trophy from his first day of hunting, and I was ready to head back to the OTO.

They were out over a month and came home with plenty of good trophies to satisfy Von Hindenburg. I was going into the high country just as June was coming out with his party. The Watsons and I were camped at the head of Jackson Lake when June pulled into camp near us. I looked up at June and his pack horses, "See you've got some nice heads there — moose, antelope, elk and more bear.... but where's Dutchy?"

"I reckon he'll be along soon ; he's gettin' pretty saddle sore," June got off his horse and tied it to a tree.

"He will, if he ain't lost again," Billy North was getting out a skillet and obviously glad this hunt was ending. "He'd been lost for good if it hadn't been for me urging June to go look for him. One night the General didn't come in and when it got dark, I says to June, 'you'd better go look for Dutchy.' 'Let him be,' June says to me, 'he's been tryin' to get lost ever since we've been on this trip.'"

"About midnight, June finally saddled up his horse and started back up the trail. He shot into the air but get no answer from Dutchy."

"That was the worst night of the whole trip," June came over to finish the story. "After I'd been ridin' for several hours, I finally saw a little flicker of light and found it was a campfire. There was Dutchy squatting down by the fire trying to roast a blue grouse, feathers and all. He had burned the side out of his fancy hunting jacket and he was one mad Dutchman. It was almost morning when I found him and all the way home he kept raving about those secret camps the guides keep hidden in the forest."

Dutchy had been told many times that a pack outfit never stops during a day's travel, except occasionally to adjust a pack. We also told him that if he ever did drop out of the string, to just give his horse his head and he would find the way back to camp. We were never able to convince Von Hindenburg that a horse could find camp even though he couldn't.

Dutchy finally rode into camp, and I went over to meet him. The horses knew the hunt was over and they were glad to be on the way home. His horse had brought him into camp.

We sat down on a log while he told me about the trip; he was pleased with the trophies he had to take home. "Mr. Buzzell was a good guide and a good hunter, but Mr. Randall, I don't understand him. When I killed a big bull elk, I was so elated, I rushed up to Mr. Buzzell, threw my arms around him and kissed him...and he knocked me down!"

"Now, General," I said, "don't think hard of June. He has always been gun-shy of women and I don't suppose he has ever been kissed before, unless by his mother."

I can imagine the Von Hindenburg line got a pretty hard fall from that 190-pound Buzzell. June stood well over six feet, had straight black hair, high cheek bones and some Indian blood. He was raised over by the Sioux nation. Most times, June was pretty good natured, but after that no one dared say, "You let a Dutchman kiss you," unless ready to run.

"I invited the General over to our camp. He was hesitant to come because he didn't feel he was presentable since there was a lady in our camp. But he finally came and we had a pleasant evening talking about big game.

Dick told that story many times as he sat with guests around a mountain campfire or in front of the fireplace in the Lodge. Quite often he followed it up with the Watson's trip:

I was glad to have June take out the General; Mr. and Mrs.
Watson were easier to hunt with. I had hunted them before and
knew there was no buck fever in this family. I remembered
when Mrs. Watson met up with a good sized grizzly. It was one of
those times when the bear had the advantage. He was on a steep
hillside and we were below him. In that situation, if your shot
isn't a death shot, you're in for trouble. Well, Mrs. Watson pulled
up her gun and put one shot into him. That stopped him for a
minute and then he started down toward us. She placed two
more shots, one in his shoulder and one in his heart. Can't tell
me women lose their nerve in dangerous situations.

We were camped that time on a little creek at the upper end
of Jackson Hole. It was a camp we always hated to leave, with a
view of the Grand Tetons and of Mt. Moran; some of America's
finest scenery. Years ago, it was hard country to get into and not
very safe. Jackson Hole was famous for its train robbers and
horse thieves. In fact, it was a hideout for a notorious gang of
outlaws. Today tourists just drive in on oiled roads for an easy
view of those 14,000 foot peaks in the Tetons.

One night while camping there, we had our 30 head of pack
and saddle horses grazing peacefully in a little meadow. I was
busy making a campfire when all of a sudden every horse's head
went up. First I thought they had caught the scent of bear. Then
the horses began to nicker, and I said to Mr. Watson, 'I think
June Buzzell and his pack string must be comin'. These horses
act like they heard the bell. June had some strange horses in his
string and he wanted to educate them to the bell. That's how
come we didn't have a bellmare with us this time. One of my
dudes had a foundry man in Switzerland make that bell for me
years ago, and every horse we own is crazy about it. There've
been times when a few horses have strayed from the bunch in
heavy timber country. The best way to locate them is to take the
bell from the picketed bellmare and go back along the trail
swinging that bell. They can hear the bell from a long ways off
and will always come at the sound of it. Pretty soon, then, you
will hear a nicker from the lost horses and they will come in

sight. A good bellmare is mighty important on a pack trip.

While I was still telling them about the bell, June and his pack string rode into camp.

I reminded the Watsons about June kissing the General; they knew June from other hunting trips and kidded him just a little. He was on his way south to the best big game hunting in the country.

A VERY SPECIAL KIND
OF FRIENDSHIP

The OTO continued to grow from that beginning in 1898 when Dick bought some pasture land that had once been a Robbers Roost, and he and Dora filed as homesteaders. They bought adjoining railroad land, leased forest land, raised cattle and horses, and managed over 5,000 acres. It was this unspoiled corner of Western Montana that became the state's first dude ranch, and Easterners came in ever increasing numbers to spend their summers in the West.

Most of the work expanding and improving the place was done by members of the family. Clyde Erskine recalls:

> The first thing I did was improve the road up Cedar Creek canyon. The road had a bad mud hole, and often it was hard, if not impossible, to get through, so I moved the road over to the other side of Cedar Creek. I had to clear logs and rocks along the creek by blasting and using a heavy hammer. It was all pick and shovel work. There was a rocky point that had to be blasted before I could put the road through. It took all winter to make that road, but for the first time we had a road with turnouts for passing. There were 14 pole bridges in that one and one half miles as the road wound down the canyon back and forth across Cedar Creek. When the road was finished, we could bring dudes into the ranch in cars.
>
> In the spring, I put private baths in two of the cabins. The Governor was very much opposed to that idea. He said people came here to rough it, and they wouldn't want a bathroom built into their cabin. He always set out a big wash-tub full of water on sunny side of the house and the water in that got warm enough

59

for bathing, according to his ideas. Guests carried it by the bucketfull into their cabins. But I kept after the Governor and finally Mother Randall and I convinced him some dudes might like a bathroom. I pointed out we were charging $35 a week, which included a good saddle horse, room and board. With a bathroom, I figured we could charge $90 single or $150 double. Very soon the "luxury" cabins were filled all the time. The Governor just shook his head; he couldn't believe people would pay extra for such foolishness. I also installed two bathrooms in the north wing of the Lodge, but it was hard to do; we had to knock out part of the foundation and make a manhole for the sewage line. I used a trench shovel to remove all that dirt. When more cabins were built, I tried to get the Governor to put bathrooms in while they were going up, but he wouldn't go for it.

The next building put up was a shower house with eight stalls and a laundry room at one end. Here we took care of all laundry, including the guests'. We had a 1,000 gallon hot water tank that we got from Army Surplus. We bought the fire bricks from an old coke oven dismantled at Devil's Slide about nine miles from the ranch. The grates were made from old railroad tracks cut in three foot lengths and there was a large space underneath for ashes. I tried to heat the tank with direct heat but that did not work, so we got some pipe, made coils and put them under the tank and built a big fire in the firebox. For awhile I thought it was going to blow up. We had hot water even in the cold water line. I knew where there was a governor on an abandoned threshing machine, so we salvaged it and put it on the water system. That did the trick, and we always had hot water with only two loadings of the firebox. Corlin Hale, a guest from Ohio, had learned to use an acetyline torch in the Army and he helped with the welding.

Members of the family continued to do all the building and most of the work. Dudes very often helped.

We built a big ice-house and I hauled ice from the river about ten miles from the ranch. We cut about three tons of ice into big chunks and loaded it on the truck. Then we got sawdust from an old sawmill and packed the chunks of ice in it. We made a "California Cooler" on the inside of the ice house and circulation past the chunks of ice kept this cool even in the hottest weather.

Mother Randall and I made about 200 pounds of cheese a year. We kept this in the runway to the ice house. Every morning while it was being made, we had to rub down the cheese. In the spring we made up about 300 pounds of butter and put it in brine. We would buy eggs from ranchers when prices were down and put them in brine; these were used for baking only. During summer we bought fresh eggs to serve for breakfast. Most canned goods were purchased in wholesale lots from a firm in Chicago, shipped out in carload lots with that of the Yellowstone Park hotels. It amounted to about three truckloads a year. All meat products, vegetables, and cheese were processed at the ranch.

We put up a small building for the power house, where we had a generator that supplied electricity, powered by a water-driven turbine. Water taken from the creek ran over a large penstock and then strained into a fourteen inch pipe, finally driving the turbine. We even sawed logs with that turbine power.

Dude ranch vacations caught on and dude ranching became a lucrative business and a way of making a cattle ranch pay. The OTO kept building and expanding to meet a growing guest list. More horses and saddles and a system of coordinating them became necessary.

Next to go up was a two-story log building called the saddle room. Upstairs was space for storage and a workshop. Along the walls downstairs were pegs and racks, with a blackboard next to the door. Each peg was numbered. The blackboard held names of guests and opposite each was the name of his horse and the number of his saddle. The bridle always hung on the saddle horn. This system made it possible to keep things in order and match up horse, rider and equipment.

A big door led from the saddle room to a cutting corral where horses were brought each morning. We would cut them out about ten at a time and run them into a smaller corral where cowboys would put on saddles and tie each horse to the hitching rack. We could get 50 horses ready for riders in 30 minutes.

At the end of the day when the dude riders came in, they would bring their horses to the corral. A cowboy would take the horse to the saddle room, unsaddle it and place all the equipment on the proper peg. Most of the time young dude boys would help; we found many eager to be helpful.

We were getting many requests to take large parties of teen-agers, both boys and girls, on the 14 day trip around the Loop in the Park, and also to stay at the ranch. We built a large two-story dormitory across the creek from the cabins. Here we could accommodate 18 guests, the girls upstairs and the boys on the ground floor. Young people loved this dorm.

I personally cut all the logs for those two buildings and dragged them down from the side of the mountain. After being felled, the logs were trimmed and cut to desired length. They were then snaked down one by one to where we could load them on our sled. The large end of the log was put on the sled and the other end dragged in the snow. We could haul six to nine logs a load, depending on size. The logs were put up to form the walls by using a pulley, a tripod, and a rope pulled by horses. We put up one layer at a time, notching each log before putting it in place.

The dudes left at the end of summer; some hunters stayed throught the fall season, but winter months found only members of the Randall family and possibly a hired man at the ranch. It was hardly a time for relaxing, however, because there was the year's wood supply to get in. Heater, the cook stove, and fireplaces required a tremendous amount. Trees were cut, trimmed, and piled in stacks before the snows came. Then, when there was snow enough for a sled, I dragged the logs down to the ranch and cut them into desired lengths. After the green wood froze, it could be split easily and put in piles to dry. It took about 20 cords of wood to see the OTO through a season. Other chores included feeding cattle, weaning calves, breaking young horses to halter and to ride. Cows were milked, butter and cheese made. But it was a change of pace from summer, and the winter days were short.

The quiet winters were only for a few years. The OTO was becoming a close knit family group that included not only the Randalls and Erskines but also guests who were coming back year after year. A very special kind of friendship grew up between dude ranchers and their guests, not only at the OTO, but at other ranches as well. Dudes came to have a real sense of belonging, of loyalty and of kinship to each other and to the dude ranchers.

OTO dudes began insisting that the Randalls and the Erskines come East and visit them. These trips and contacts took the West to the East and opened a whole new method of promotion for the OTO. Outgoing, genuine people that they were, these Westerners found themselves as comfortable in New York as in Montana, and it was a delightful change for a few weeks each year.

Dick was a popular speaker at Rotary Clubs, at Chamber of Commerce luncheons, at the Men's Clubs in cities where his summer guests lived. He was a natural-born entertainer and story teller.

The Evening Repository of Canton, Ohio, had headlines: "Noted Hunter Addresses McKinley High Pupils," and went on to report.

> Dick Randall, who shot bears with Roosevelt, holds students spellbound with tales of the Wild West and bear hunts. Randall was in Canton Monday and in the afternoon told the students of McKinley High School his best bear stories. He held his audience enthralled for an hour and responded with a bow to one of the most enthusiastic encores ever accorded a lecturer here.

The *St. Paul Sunday Pioneer Press* headlines for March 4, 1928 were, "Bronco Bustin' Pioneer Tells How the West Does It."

> Dick Randall, adventuresome friend of presidents and millionaires would rather break colts three times a day than to ride in limousines....Cow-puncher, bronco buster, stage coach driver, vigilante, big game hunter, guide, and friend to presidents and members of the Four Hundred, successful rancher....snow white hair, pink and white complexion, blue eyes that can look through a mountain, physique like a lightweight boxer...a grandfather with the spirit and carriage of a boy. That, in brief, is Dick Randall, pioneer of the Rocky Mountain cow country, who has been visiting friends in St. Paul the past few days on his annual winter pilgrimage from the old homestead in Montana (a 5,000

acre ranch) to the effete East. Accompanied by Mrs. Randall, he will spend several weeks in New York and other Eastern cities where live the millionaires and millionairesses who have visited the Randalls in Montana.

The *Boston Evening Transcript* for March 26, 1932 ran a full page feature of photos and information about the OTO:

Easterners more and more find a new pleasure in discipline and discover beauty in the wild landscape of Rocky Mountain peaks and rolling grasslands. ...Only in America and only in the West can you live this kind of life....It is known as dude ranching, and if you live east of the Mississippi, you are known as a dude even if you were the heaviest fullback Harvard ever had...Dude ranching is the institution which puts you on the back of a horse at 6 o'clock in the morning and leads you up through mountain mists over a rocky trail into a world turning rosy and golden in the morning sun. It takes you by devious ways along rock rims or over vast rolling country into new, seemingly untrodden worlds. It gives you aches in the back and chafed places on the legs; it gives you new appreciation for the bed at night and for the taste of bacon, biscuits and coffee. For city dwellers, it is a renascence. By buying a Pullman ticket, a man is translated into an existence without familiar landmarks. He becomes a subject in the realm of the horse. He learns again some of the humility he may have lost. He is glad to put himself under the tutelage of an old hand....On a ranch and on a horse, nothing is done that doesn't have a direct meaning.

In the companionship of these cowboy wranglers, an Easterner often finds a delightful friendship. When the ranchmen come East in the winter, their journey is a succession of reunions. There is no mistaking these ambassadors. If you encounter one, you'll know what he is...a strong easy set to his shoulders and a face with an even tan right down to the collar line.

***

There's more to running a dude ranch than you might think. There also has to be provision or those who come out into that horsey country with their minds only on trout streams, or the ladies who want to pick wild flowers and have no inclination to get into a saddle. There must be activities to fill up their days, too. Diplomacy as well as judgment goes into the handling of people, and Dick Randall is a master of both.

The Minneapolis Sunday Journal for March 18, 1934, has a feature story on "Veteran Rancher Laments Passing of Old Range Days. ...Dick Randall, 67, recalls wnter of heavy snows that took 90,000 of the 7 Bar 7 cattle."

New England, New York and the Mid-west were becoming aware of Montana and Wyoming dude ranches.

The Randalls built the OTO up to accommodate 100 guests, and they realized the importance of wide-spread publicity to keep the cabins full each summer.

Charlie Ritchie of Chicago was at the ranch several seasons and he and Clyde Erskine became very good friends.

"Clyde," he said one day, "my wife, our boy, and I always have a winter vacation in Florida for a couple of months. Why don't you and Bess come to Chicago and I will help you get acquainted with good prospects for the ranch; you can live in our apartment."

Clyde continues with his recorded story:

I thought it was a good idea, so when we accepted we told the Governor and Mother what we were going to do. They decided to go East to visit friends in New York, Philadelphia and Boston. We had two cowboys, Bud Wilkinson and Johnny Taylor who could look after the ranch.

At the Ritchie's apartment in the evenings, Bess often played the piano and I sang. It was the way we passed the time there and the way we entertained the dudes back at the OTO. One evening there was a knock at the door. It was our neighbor in the apartment house who had heard our music. He worked for the Chicago Tribune and wanted us to go down to their broadcasting studio to try out. It was a flattering offer, but we weren't interested in a radio career; we had our life and our work cut out for us at the OTO.

The Governor got a large movie projector that used standard film, and Bell & Howard made a film for us. The film was about activities on a dude ranch. Dick was the leading cowboy in the film; the setting was the ranch in Montana. The Governor carried this film and a display each time he went East. We had two silver-mounted saddle outfits as well as one for kids, Navajo saddle blankets and complete equipment for the horses. Dick would go into a city, choose the largest or most famous department store and rent a window for a week. He would then dress the window, and, he was good at it. He used the trappings on a paper mache horse, and mannequins for adults and children dressed in Western clothes. It always drew crowds and was good publicity. Newspapers had feature stories about the windows and the OTO Ranch; it was new and refreshing. Mother Randall and Bess would stay at the entrance to the store and handle requests for information or booking of guests. The Governor was there, oo, ready to be interviewed. At different times we had displays in Wanamakers, Marshall Fields, Jordan Marshall and others.

The Northern Pacific Railroad was also promoting the dude ranch business and travel to the West. Public relations men kept the Governor busy most of the time going to schools, churches, and clubs. He was in demand for his entertaining talks and would end up selling the West to his listeners. Sometimes Dick took helpers along to display Western clothes, or guns, or artifacts. Once he took an Indian bridal dress that had been made out of uniforms taken from soldiers on the Custer Battlefield. It was decorated with over 200 elk teeth.

One year Dick got a contest going at a radio station. He offered a prize of two weeks at the ranch. Other prizes were Stetson hats and Justin cowboy boots. Hires Company of Denver gave an outfit for a prize and chaps came from Conley Brothers in Billings. The Northern Pacific gave a ticket for transportation to and from the OTO Ranch. Out of this publicity of Dick's developed the popular "Queen for a Day" program.

***

Dude ranching, like any business, had its ups and downs. There were lean years following World War I. During one of those lean years, Clyde decided he would go into the cattle business with Dick. He borrowed money to buy the stock. The winter was tough. It got down to 40 degrees below zero at the ranch. Dick and Mrs. Randall had gone to Florida for the winter and Bess and Clyde stayed home to take care of the OTO and the cattle.

Bess set up a school at the ranch and taught the neighbor's child, two children from the Children's Home living with us, and our two nephews. There were 160 head of cattle to be fed and we couldn't afford hired help. I had a dog helping to keep the cattle from going into the pen while I fed hay out on the meadows. There were 100 calves to be fed from mangers inside the corrals, and 16 colts to be halter broke that winter; every day each one had to be led to water. Sixteen cows had to be milked morning and night and the separator cared for. We ran out of hay and bought 60 tons of alfalfa from a neighbor. Ergot infested, it caused abortion in the cattle and we lost 90 percent of our next year's calf crop.

One stack of second cutting hay had been saved for the milk cows. After we moved the cattle down river where we had bought some more hay, I went over to get the second cutting for the milk cows and found that elk had broken down the corral fence and scattered the hay over the 20 acre field. I will never forget that day. I sat down on the side of the hayrack and cried like a baby. When I told Bess, she said "Don't worry, we'll get through this." Her teaching money went to pay the interest on the loan.

Obviously, we weren't going to make any money in the cattle business and the dude season was still several months away, so we started giving dances to get money enough to carry us through the winter. We scheduled dances up and down the valley; Bess would play the piano and I would sing. One New Year's eve, there was a bunch of fellows yelling at me to sing more. They threw seventeen silver dollars to me; they looked as big as wagon wheels! At most dances, we would serve elk meat sandwiches, cake, tea, and coffee with thick cream from our own cows. We charged one dollar for this lunch and served it at midnight. Then we would play for another two or three hours of dancing. Every day that winter lasted from 5 a.m. to 10 or 11 p.m. and much later on dance nights. We had two game wardens for boarders. It took us five years to recover from our losses in the cattle venture.

*Dick Randall had just as much fun clowning for his friends
on their Eastern golf courses as he did at the OTO.*

Charles Herbert of Fox Pathe News arriving from Miami, Florida, to set up headquarters at the OTO.
The Model A Ford and Dick Randall on horseback met him at the West Yellowstone station.

Charlie Herbert making films for Fox Movietone News featured Bess at the Buckaroo.

Colonel DeOlier, his wife, daughter Anne, and son "Nank" in Atlantic City and at the OTO.

A days ride in the Absaroka Mountains near the ranch. —UM

Dudes line up on the corral fence for an impromptu ranch rodeo.
Riders will be George Randall holding the saddle on the left and
Jimmy Powers on the right, ready to put a saddle on his horse. —UM

By 1926, the streets of Livingston were lined with Model A Fords
as the Fourth of July parade led to the rodeo grounds. The OTO guests
took over the whole Park Hotel for the three days of rodeo.

Each year the dudes rode in the Fourth of July parade for the Livingston Rodeo.
Here Dick Randall and his daughter, Bess Erskine, are leading the parade.

For three years, Edwin L. Taylor (ninth from left), president of the New Haven Railroad, and his party of 17 spent their summer vacations at the OTO. They always came in time for the Livingston Rodeo and rode with the rest of the OTO dudes in the parades. This photo, taken by Brown for N.P., was taken in front of the Northern Pacific station in Livingston.

Mr. E. L. Taylor of New Haven, Connecticut, was a yearly guest at the OTO.

*The gentlemen from Maine were trying hard to get that western look.
Chan Libby who later bought the OTO and his uncle.*

A dude wrangler's dilemma. —Museum of the Rockies

Dude wranglers and pretty Eastern girls just naturally got together. Photo courtesy of George Randall.

Waiting for the dinner bell.

There's something very special about a camp fire at night in the mountains.

The Governor was a wonderful camp cook.
Dutch oven biscuits and pan-fried trout were his specialties.

Hunters began to ask if they could bring their families for a summer vacation, so Randalls built some cabins to accommodate family groups.

Practically all pack trips from the OTO went to the summit of this mountain in the Absaroka National Forest. —UM

Bess "topping off" a pony.
Only dependable and well trained
horses could be given to the dudes.

Morning wake up. George Randall at a Cedar Creek waterfall. —UM

Dick and Mother Randall went East each winter. The OTO dudes in every city entertained them and introduced them to even more people who wanted to come to Montana.

Recreation room at the OTO. Note chandelier made of a buffalo skull.

Whether it was in a high school in St. Louis or around the fire at the OTO Lodge, Dick Randall held his audience. This time he was telling them about the habits of the Rocky Mountain bear. Hartley Dodge, Jr. is at the extreme right.

It takes a little practice. —UM

DUDES, DEAR ONES
AND DIFFICULT

Much as the Randalls loved their dudes, there were some problem ones.

There was the English teacher from Cornell University, the one who had asked what to bring for evening wear. Upon arrival, Miss Martin informed Dick that she was used to riding Blue Ribbon horses and wanted no other kind. Dick chose a spirited mount for her and instructed the corral boys to have it ready in the morning. Miss Martin arrived in the barn a little early and when the boys came, they found her trying to get on the wrong side of the horse. Dick appeared on the scene and sized up the situation immediately, "Boys, you heard me wrong, it's Bill we want to get in for this lady to ride, not Nick." So gentle old Bill was saddled for her, but each time she rode the cowboys had to help Miss Martin get on her horse. The cowboys kept playing tricks on her because she pretended to know so much more than she really did. One day they braided blue ribbons in her horse's mane and tail.

"You get that out of there!" Dick said when he saw it. "Poor old Bill is getting downright embarrassed." The next night the cowboys got behind her cabin and howled like coyotes. That scared her and she left. "Miss Martin was one of the few misfits we ever had at the ranch."

Clyde remembers one couple that Mother and the Governor had booked for the summer.

They seemed like a nice business couple, but one night, at the cocktail hour, the man got to telling me that he was having trouble back home and had to move out of Chicago. It developed he had once belonged to a gang and had done something they didn't like, so they were after him. He was at the ranch hiding out. We got busy and sent them on a pack trip into the mountains with the understanding that they would leave the OTO as soon as the trip was over. We didn't want a gang shoot-out on our place.

The second year the Ritchies came from Chicago they brought a couple from St. Louis with them. The lady's name was Pauline and she was a lovely lady, but she had never ridden a horse until a couple of weeks before coming to Montana. She had taken a few lessons at a riding stable.

The second day at the ranch, she went with a group for a two-hour ride. When she came back, she asked the Governor, "How do I look in my saddle?"

The Governor, sort of caught off guard, gave his honest opinion. "Just like a sack of flour tied in the middle."

Poor Pauline turned on her heels, went to the Ritchie's cabin and announced that she was leaving. Mrs. Ritchie said, "But the Governor wants to make a good rider of you, Pauline; this is his way of telling you!" Mrs. Ritchie invited Dick to her cabin for cocktails at five that evening and he went straight to Pauline, "I wouldn't hurt your feelings for the world, but I'm going to make you a good rider, as we did Mrs. Ritchie last year." From then on Pauline and the Governor were good friends and by the time she left at the end of the summer, she was a good rider and a loyal OTO dude.

We tried having different types of "cowboys" for guiding dudes. We started taking college boys and thought they would work out well during summer vacations, but they did not. Then we got Leonard Bloodworth and his wife; he was the champion cowboy at Madison Square Garden one year, and his wife a saddle horse trick rider. They did guiding for us and entertained the guests by putting on trick riding and roping shows in the ranch corral. At least one evening a week, the dudes would all line up on the corral fence and yell their heads off as the cowboys, and especially the Bloodworths, put on little rodeos. The Bloodworths and the dudes rode in the big parades for us and this was good advertising, too.

Then we finally came around to hiring people who had been guests at our ranch. We knew their ability handling horses and people. This worked very well; they knew what dudes wanted and they knew the country from previous summers at the ranch.

***

Charlie Herbert, who was making full-length features and free-lance pictures for Fox Movietone News, arrived at the ranch to make a moving picture. He wanted a mechanical contraption that would buck like a horse.

Clyde set out to invent a Dude Ranch version of the Wooden Horse.

The more we worked with it, the more complicated it became. Finally, we took a 20 inch diameter tree, cut a piece out about three feet long, axed it out to make a place for the saddle, so it would sit much as it does on a horse. Holes were drilled with a two inch bit, about six or eight inches deep and at an angle of some 45 degrees. Into each hole went a stick about 2½ inches in diameter, one cut off at about 30 inches above the log, the other, the neck, left a little longer and tied with a pillow on the end for a head. The head was fastened securely with a rope which served as reins for the rider. Lag screws with eyes were put in each of the four corners of the log with a pull rope tied to each; the ropes were about 18 feet long and strung twelve feet apart at the outer ends. At the end of these, we set posts at a slant and tied ropes securely to them.

The guests were delighted to man the ropes whenever we got a "cowboy" in the saddle. By pulling on diagonal ropes and alternating corner pulls, the contraption would get to swinging like a bucking horse. Then, pulling the tail rope, the wooden horse went into a tail spin and dislodged any rider.

"Now that we've got it," Charlie said, "what shall we call it?"

I suggested "Buckaroo." As far as I know it was the first one made and named, though several variations have been made

71

since. We had fun with it and the dudes just couldn't leave it alone. One day Mr. Herbert came to me and said, "I've got an idea. I want Bess to ride the Buckaroo while I take some pictures for Fox Movietone News." The result was a winner; it went all over the United States.

Most of our guests were interested in real horseback riding but everyone got a laugh or two out of watching people on our Wooden Horse.

While Charlie Herbert made the OTO Ranch his headquarters, he took animal pictures for the Fox weekly feature. Within easy range were deer, coyote, bear, porcupine, and sheep, which soon appeared on screens across the nation. Our dudes enjoyed watching the filming and quite often they, too, got in the picture. One night we got pictures of a porcupine raiding Mother Randall's garden. We rounded up four porcupines and put them under tubs until Charlie was ready to shoot. I handled them with gauntlet gloves and wore a heavy elk-skin suit so the quills would not touch my body. We set the tubs in the garden with the "porks" underneath them. When Charlie was ready to photograph the porcupines, we lifted the tubs and ran them out of camera range. Charlie took several shots of the porcupines and the pictures turned out so well he got $500 for them; in those days that was big money.

We captured two badgers and penned them up until Charlie was ready to take their pictures. They are quick and vicious little devils, but we managed to get some dandy shots of them.

Charlie wanted pictures of coyotes, so we raided a den and took two pups down to the ranch. We fed them for a month and put them on a leash tied to the clothesline so they could run back and forth for exercise. They seemed tame, and a couple from Pasadena later took them home, but they attacked a small child and had to be destroyed. Coyotes are wild creatures and should be left in the wild.

We tried to make a pet of a bear, too. Ours seemed gentle and Charlie was able to get good photos. We kept him tied on a leash and a small chain. He loved milk warm from the separator. One day he broke loose and started for the tall timber with his chain and collar on. Bess discovered he was gone and knew he might get hung up on something with that chain. She got on her horse and took out after the bear. She finally found him high in a tree and after some time was able to get to him and take the collar and chain off. He headed for the woods and we never saw him again.

We kept a few bum lambs at the ranch and fed them with a nipple on a catsup bottle. The dudettes (what we called the dude children) loved to feed the lambs, and some of Charlie's most appealing pictures were of these city children holding bottles for eager little lambs gulping down milk and wagging their tails. Herbert got some good prize money for those pictures.

"Shakey" was our pet pig. One of the cowboys found him, newborn and almost dead from the cold. He brought him into the house; Bess rolled the shaking little pig in a blanket and put him in a box by the stove. We kept him inside until he was strong enough to be in the pen with the others. Even months later when we called, Shakey would come to the fence to greet us.

This was the silent side of dude ranching. These animals had to be cared for year round and were an important part of the economy of the ranch; they were also an attraction for city dudes. We ran a large herd of cattle, milk cows, pigs, and some 300 horses for riding and farm work. In the city Movietone News showed pictures of domestic and wild animals to acquaint children with them. Such exposure is now in every child's home through television. It was not so in the 1920's.

***

One time we thought it would be fun and a thrill for our dudes if we staged a hold-up down in the canyon. We arranged it so Charlie Herbert could take movies of the action. We let very few people know what we had in mind, because we wanted it to be a surprise and as realistic as possible for our guests. Charlie was to be stationed with his camera at a point where the people could not see him. The Governor was to drive the four-horse team and coach loaded with dudes, timed to arrive in the canyon about 3:30 p.m. so the light would be right for Charlie's pictures. We had a couple of our wranglers, complete with masks,

73

stationed there to pull the "hold-up." I stood behind a big boulder to watch for anything that might be dangerous. An outsider happening by could cause a lot of problems.

The stage was set: The Governor had his stagecoach full of dudes, driving the four-horse team lickety-split down the canyon, and the "hold-up" men with guns raised were at their stations. Just as Charlie gave the signal for action, two strangers did come riding by. They were cowhands on horseback and they jumped at the chance to rescue the travelers. They pulled out guns and ordered our wranglers to drop their guns and stand back. I spotted the trouble and came down with my rifle cocked. I explained the situation and told the two strangers to get the hell out of there, but the plan was foiled. We never again tried staging a hold-up for dudes.

One other trip turned out to be a fiasco, too, though for a very different reason. During the summer of 1929, I had been at the ranch only three nights, spending most of the time with Bess in the hills. It was the last part of August and Bess and I were just getting in from a long trip through Yellowstone Park. We had hardly landed at the ranch when the Governor told me he had planned another trip for Bess and me; to take a man, his wife and four-year-old son to a high mountain camp at 11,000 ft. They were from Philadelphia and had never been on a camping trip; and we soon found they were very poor riders. But the Governor had promised them a mountain trip, and that was that!

We left the ranch at noon the next day, and landed at Knox Lake about dusk. I hurried to gather wood so Bess could start cooking supper. I pulled the packs off, and then put the horses out to pasture with hobbles on. The tents had to be put up quickly because a storm was brewing and I knew we were going to have a rough night. This dude and his wife were no help at all; they never should have left Philadelphia. During the night it started to rain and by the time we crawled out in the morning, everything was soaking wet. By 7 o'clock I managed to get a fire going by gathering pine needles from under heavy tree limbs and sparking them with pitch.

When we went to check the horses, not one was in sight. Hobbles and all, they had started for home, as animals often will

74

when a storm is coming. I started out on foot and was able to catch up with them on top of the Divide. It was two o'clock in the afternoon when I got back to camp with those horses. I was tired, disgusted and hungry.

Later that afternoon a small black cub bear wandered into camp; out ran this dude with a 22 rifle ready to shoot the poor little feller. I let out a yell and chased the cub bear away. The dude was more scared than the bear. I asked what in hell he planned to do. He said he had always wanted to kill a bear. I took his gun away and told him he had endangered our lives because the mother bear was undoubtedly very near and would have torn us to pieces if he had wounded the cub.

The little boy was shivering, cold and miserable. They had not brought proper clothes for him. He was crying and the parents didn't seem to know what to do except scold him. I picked him up and carried him piggy back for at least an hour. That pleased him and he felt better.

We had had enough of this trip, so I started to break camp, planning to get an early start out the next morning. I made a rope corral and put the horses in it for the night. The rain had stopped and we had gotten things dry and comfortable but we could see these people were never going to make it as campers.

We were up at 6 a.m. getting breakfast and packing the horses. We told the dudes to pack their things, because we were going back to the ranch. We arrived there about 2 p.m. and the man went to the office, paid his bill with a check for about $600. They left on the evening train. The check bounced and we never did get anything for their stay at the ranch or that miserable pack trip.

***

There were so many interesting and delightful guests at the OTO that it was easy to forget the difficult ones. Like the time when two young men in a fancy sports car stopped at the ranch and said they would like to go for a horseback ride. We seldom took unscheduled and unknown guests but they seemed eager and friendly, so I told them we would give them a horse they could handle but first they should take a test on our Buckaroo. They did and had a lot of fun. We gave them good horses and they went for a long ride. When they came back they said they would like to stay for a few days.

They were French boys who were touring America. After dinner we went into the lounge; Bess played the piano, I sang and the boys joined in. We found they were delightful entertainers. One was the son of the European banker, Rothchild, and the other was from a wealthy French family. He was a real clown and especially enjoyed imitating Maurice Chevalier. Another of our guests came in while we were singing and recognized his friend, Rothchild; they had a happy reunion. The boys stayed ten days and we had great evenings of entertainment while they were with us.

I remember the Harlan Davis family, too. They brought a nurse with them to care for their six-month-old son, so Lolo Davis could spend more time riding her pony. She was a good rider and loved the out-of-doors. The nurse would go to the garden each morning with Mother Randall and select the very best vegetables to cook for the baby; she always took spinach, potatoes, and carrots. Every day she cooked them all together and mashed them up. She put young Harlan in the high chair and started poking the mash down him. He would yell at the top of his voice and we could hear him all over the ranch. The next day, it was the same vegetables and the same protest. No change in his diet and no change in his yelling. In 1976, Harlan, now a Chicago business man, came to see us. He had his grown son with him. We asked, "Do you still like carrots and spinach?" He let out a yell, and we all had a good laugh over those vegetables the nurse tried to poke down him so many happy years ago.

The Braun family of Detroit spent two months with us in the summer of 1922. They had a stable of 14 horses at home, so all were excellent riders. Mr. and Mrs. Braun rode in fox-hunts back in Michigan and their five children rode, too. Mrs. Braun had a beautiful riding habit which she wore on a trip we took to a mountain lake. I went with her to teach her how to fish. This was her first experience, and she worked hard at learning the technique. Finally she hooked a one-pound brook trout. While she was pulling the fish out, it got off the hook and landed in a small pool a short distance from the main water. Mrs. Braun dropped her pole and went in after that fish with her bare hands. She emerged 15 minutes later, her beautiful green riding habit dripping wet, but in her hand was the fish and on her face a look of triumph. "I got the little son-of-a-gun," she announced and held it up for us to see.

While Dick was in New York City one year, he met a diamond broker, and the following summer the broker and a companion showed up at the ranch. They wanted to go into the hills for a week's pack trip and we arranged it for them. On the day we were to start, they brought a traveling case to Dick and asked him to care for it while they were away. He told the men he had no safe to keep valuables in and asked what they had in the case. "Diamonds," they said, "but it'll be all right; just toss the case under Mother Randall's bed.

Dick was not about to assume responsibility for such valuables so he said "You'd better take the case down to the Express office in Livingston where they have a safe." The men protested that they didn't have time, but Dick insisted. They went to Livingston on the train, and we delayed the pack trip for a day until they got back. After they had gone, Dick said to me, "You never know who are crooks and who are honest. Some other people might have known about the diamonds and Mother could have been in danger."

Superintendent Horace Albright of Yellowstone Park recommended our ranch to Colonel Franklin D'Olier, then president of the Prudential Insurance Company. He was also Commander of the American Legion. Their party consisted of the Colonel, Mrs. D'Olier and their three children, Ellie, Ann, and Franklin Jr., called "Nank." The Colonel wanted his family to see how people lived in the West. We had just finished building the big Lodge and had stretched our finances as far as they would go, so the cabins remained rustic. There were few conveniences of any kind. One day I heard the Colonel laughing and found him with Ellie, his nine-year-old daughter, both busily washing their clothes in the creek. The water was hard, cold, and even a bit murky, but there they were trying hard to rough it. Mr. D'Olier thought it would be a good idea if Ann helped in the kitchen, so every evening after supper, 17-year-old Ann could be seen helping wash the dishes. Nank returned to our ranch for several seasons, always a most welcome guest, and later an excellent guide for us.

The Colonel was a close friend of Franklin Roosevelt. When they were young, they had gone to the same school. He told us of the different ways Franklin did things and that he thought Roosevelt would be president some day. That was in 1922. During the 1932 election year, I was managing Old Faithful Lodge in Yellowstone Park and Nank D'Olier was working at the ranch hauling people back and forth and acting as a guide. They all said Roosevelt didn't have a chance to be elected, — one guest even commenting that he was as crippled above the hips as below. That was the first time I had known of Roosevelt's paralysis. "Tell you one thing, though," continued my prophetic friend, "if Roosevelt does get elected, his old lady will wear the pants and we'll also get a woman in the cabinet...Secretary of Labor, I'm predicting."

When Colonel D'Olier was at the ranch, he liked to hear Dick tell stories of the early days and of exciting hunts. When the Randalls travelled to New York in the winter, D'Olier always spent two or three days taking the Governor around and introducing him to friends. Dick said he had to take the West back East to get people interested.

One year, Dick was contacted by Mrs. Hartley (Rockefeller) Dodge; she wanted to book Hartley Dodge, Jr., his companion and her dog man for a full summer in the mountains. The Governor promised to handle the party himself, and to help them hunt bear and other big game available within the law. By then there were game laws in Montana.

The Dodge party arrived on the Northern Pacific, and we went to Corwin Springs to meet them. I drove the truck for the baggage. One of the wranglers took the Governor; he always greeted special guests and met them at the train. When we put the baggage in the truck, Hartley Dodge, Sr. came over and asked if he could ride with me to the ranch. I said, "of course," and all along the way he was full of questions. When we landed at the

OTO, got the baggage sorted and the party registered, Hartley Dodge Sr. disappeared. He showed up later for lunch and said he had looked over the whole place. He just wanted to be sure his son would be in good hands and that everything was in order.

Before the scheduled pack trip with young Dodge, his father asked if it would be possible for Bess and me to take him up to Knox Lake for a few days ahead of the main party. He wanted to see how things would be in the mountains, but didn't want the month-long trip. We took him up and camped for three days; Dodge was satisfied that OTO personnel could handle a hunting trip for his son.

When we got back to the ranch, Dodge was pleased to see his son had taken up target shooting even though he was using up half a case of ammunition a day. The father said he had tried to get his son interested in this for a long time, but until he came West, he wouldn't do it. He joked with Dick about it and said maybe he'd have to go back and put an addition on his Remington Arms factory.

The pack trip with young Dodge, and with Halley, his bodyguard, Applegate, his friend, and the dog man was a big success. They were out 30 days and came home with trophies, stories of adventure and giant appetites. When the Governor went to New York the following winter, Mrs. Dodge started giving him a bad time about letting Hartley, Jr. ride a wild steer. The Governor said, "Well, he rode him, didn't he? Hartley is a real boy and you should be proud of him."

She smiled, "I am."

The steer riding happened at the Livingston Rodeo. Young Dodge was staying close to Dick and kept asking if he could try riding a steer. The Governor asked Kramer, who was head of the rodeo, if he could find a steer for Dodge to ride. Kramer and Randall finally got young Dodge into a chute and showed him how to grab the rope and let him in on a few tricks that helped in riding a steer. When the announcement came that Hartley Dodge, Jr. was coming out of Chute #3, Hartley Sr. grabbed his seat; but before he had time to protest, out came his son on a bucking steer. He stayed on for a few seconds and then hit the wire fence right in front of his father as the steer gave a lunge and ran out from under him. Young Hartley picked himself off the ground, looked up into the bleachers and said, "Hi, Dad."

While Hartley Dodge, Sr. was at the ranch, he got up every morning at 4 o'clock and walked to the horse pasture. He would rope one of the dude horses, put a bridle on, and ride bareback to help the wranglers bring the string in for the day's ride.

Dodge had a fine sense of humor, too, and made friends easily around the ranch. Ralph Hemming of Washington D.C., with his wife and daughter, were coming to spend some time at the OTO. He was with the Chicago Tribune at the time, and scheduled to arrive on the morning train. I was leaving the Lodge to meet the Hemmings at the station when Dodge came running out and asked if he could ride in with me. I said, "Sure, there's plenty of room." We drove to the station and pulled in just as the train was coming in. I jumped out and went to the platform so I would be there to greet our guests when they stepped from the train.

I met the guests, loaded their luggage in the truck and escorted them to the car. There stood Hartley Dodge with all the doors open. I did not introduce him because I could see he was having so much fun pretending. He bowed and closed the doors after the Hemmings got in. He was dressed in clothes like a cow poke: faded Levis, run-over cowboy boots, a faded pink shirt and an old battered Stetson. We arrived at the ranch and I started to take the new dudes to the Lodge.

"What rooms do they have?" Hartley asked and I told him. When we finished registering, Hartley bowed again and proceeded to put luggage in the rooms. He raised the windows and went through all the standard bell-boy tricks, but when Mr. Hemming reached into his pocket for change, Hartley got out quickly.

Mrs. Hemming asked if we dressed for dinner and we told her no, she could come just as she was. I suggested she and her husband come at 5:45, so we could introduce them to the other guests. She asked if a Mr. Dodge from New York was there, and I said, "Yes, he's around somewhere." She then asked if it could be arranged for him to sit with them at dinner. When we came into the dining room, Hartley Sr. was still dressed in his faded

Levis and was leaning against the piano. Mrs. Hemming asked if the "help" ate with the guests. I didn't answer, but went on introducing her to other dudes. Then I called Dodge and said, "Come on over and meet the Hemmings." He came with a big grin, and Mrs. Hemming almost fainted as he said, "Hi Ralph, we were in the same class at Princeton...remember?"

Each summer we took our dudes to the Livingston Rodeo, July 2nd, 3rd, and 4th. We trailed about 100 head of horses fifty miles to Livingston. Dudes who wanted to, could help. We spent the first night at Chico Hot Springs and went on into Livingston the next day. The OTO party usually took half the rooms at the old Park Hotel, but sometimes filled every room. The manager let us use part of the dining room for dancing, and Bess and a couple of the boys would furnish music for the evening.

Our horses were kept at the old Harvet Ranch about half-a-mile from the Rodeo grounds. Dick and Mother always rode in the parade with the dudes. Bess and I took care of the horses, getting up at 4 a.m. to feed them before having our own hearty breakfast at the hotel. That meal had to last until 7 o'clock in the evening. After breakfast we would go to the corral, catch the horses, saddle them, and have them ready for the riders and the 10 o'clock parade. At noon, Bess and I would hold the horses in the corral and have them ready for the dudes to ride over to the Rodeo grounds again after lunch, in time for the Grand Entry. When that was over, Bess and I took the horses back to the Harvet Ranch and unsaddled them. We could sometimes get back to the Rodeo just about the time "Old Earthquake" would come out. He was a big work horse no one had been able to ride. For several years, he was the main feature of the day, scheduled to be the last horse out of the chutes. On the last day, after the Grand Entry, we pulled the saddles off the horses and Bess with one of the wranglers would start them down the road for home. The horses could make that 50 mile trip in six or seven hours when they knew they were headed home. I would load the saddles in the truck and head for the OTO, glad the job was over for another year. The dudes who had ridden horses on the trip in were tired now, too, and glad to ride home in the ranch cars.

CAMPING IN THE HIGH COUNTRY

They were world's apart, those offices at the Chase Manhattan Bank in New York City and the rustic cabins at the OTO. It took Dick Randall and others like him to bridge the gap and open the Western way of living to executives from Eastern Cities. Dude ranch vacations could be quiet and leisurely with only occasional horseback rides into the mountains, or they could be rugged and adventurous. Pack trips into the high country had to be scheduled and planned well in advance, for Montana summer seasons were short and snow lay deep on the trails until June.

July and August were the best months for pack trips, and from the OTO they usually started right after the big Fourth of July Rodeo at Livingston. Dick preferred to take at least a month for a pack trip, "A man gets the feel of the mountains when he's out that long." Put a sack of flour, coffee, dry beans and a few slabs of bacon on the pack horse and Dick could make out on any camping trip. "Anybody ought to be able to live off the land with all this game to pick from." It was a new experience for men used to having steaks served with all the flourishes at their private Clubs to find themselves faced with a haunch of venison and a hunting knife for the prospect of a meal. A good appetite and Dick's way with food on a camp fire soon made "mountain men" out of city dwellers.

OTO horses knew the trail as well as the men did. One-horse wide, the trail wound up the mountainside, through tall timber, crossing and recrossing Cedar Creek heading for the Continental Divide. Dick rode the lead horse calling to his guests to acquaint them with this fresh new world of nature. "See that cliff over there;

man or horse couldn't hang on any place, but mountain sheep can run up and down like it was a highway. Some seasons of the year, you can see a dozen or more on that mountainside." Often a deer or a game bird darted in front of the riders. "Deer are natural browsers, long as there's quakin' asp trees; they can thrive."

Men and horses had to rest occasionally as the pack train neared the top and the air thinned. The view from the top was breathtaking. Standing on the Divide a person could look in all directions and drink in the West at her majestic best: the jagged peaks of Yellowstone Park, spectacular needle points of the Tetons and the massive ranges of the Absorakas. A field of glacial ice spread out before the travellers gave promise of water for low-land streams, and a mile of precarious travel as the horses would carefully edge their way across.

"No matter how many times I come up here," Dick would comment, "there's a thrill to standing on a mountain top; makes a man feel like he can conquer anything." The dudes came to feel that way, too. Corporation worries and city traffic faced as Easterners breathed in the mountain atmosphere and let their eyes roam across the mountains.

Later, riders were in for a jolting ride as each horse picked his way down precarious, narrow trails and over slide rock. After a four mile downhill ride, shimmering Knox Lake was a welcome sight to saddle-sore dudes. Nestled in a canyon and full of fish, this lake was a favorite of all who came. "Places like this take care of a man's soul as well as his body," Dick would say as he bustled about catching fish for supper and getting the camp fire started. After a day in camp, dudes became ardent fishermen and had trout ready for breakfast each morning.

Randall established a permanent camp near Knox Lake and often Bess and Clyde stayed there while a guide from the ranch brought the dudes in and out. The guides shuttled back and forth about once a week, bringing in needed supplies and mail as well as guests. These pack and camping trips were usually scheduled for two-week periods and most dudes were reluctant to leave at the end of that time. The outings became more and more popular; dudes liked the trail ride, the scenery, the fishing and especially evenings around a campfire. Always there was singing, and it was a special treat when Dick was there to tell stories of early days in Yellowstone Park.

"How was it when you drove stage coach around the park?" some guest would ask and Dick was off on one of his stories about the excitement of driving a six-horse team pulling a passenger-loaded coach around those narrow mountain roads.

"Now, one time," he might begin, "there'd been a washout and a big tree fell across the road. I always carried an axe, so the men got down and took a turn at hacking away at the tree. That was no problem but right across the creek bed, there stood two old cow moose with calves. Now a cow moose ain't somethin you lock horns with if you can help it, and they was lookin' like they thought we was intrudin' on private pasture. It took a good two hours to get the tree moved and by then the ladies was askin' for a comfort stop; but there ain't much comfort in a stop with a cow moose breathin' down your neck. To top it off, just as the ladies was steppin' down on the far side of the coach, what should come amblin' out of the trees but a cinnamon bear wishin' we'd invite him to lunch. He smelled our ham sandwiches and came down for a snack. We threw him a few sandwiches and shooed the ladies back on the coach.

"Downed trees weren't as hard to handle as highway robbers, though." Dick could spin an exciting yarn about the time his coach was held up by masked bandits. And bear stories were always good for some spine-tingling because the possibility of one wandering into any camp was very real. Squealing horses in the middle of the night meant a bear had come into camp. Bears often visited the camp at Knox Lake and one time a bruin put his paw precisely in the middle of Bess's freshly baked and frosted cake.

Bears were very much a part of any Yellowstone story. Jack Denny, Clyde's packer and assistant on one trip around the Park, was sleeping in the truck bed and the first night out a squirrel jumped on his face and he let out a scream, yelling that a bear was after him as he bound out of the truck.

"That night fourteen bears did come into our camp just as we were ready to sit down to supper," recalls Clyde. "We shooed them back into the woods and assigned Jack the job of keeping a fire going all night, so the bruins would stay away from camp. Jack fell asleep; the fire went out and about 2 a.m. an old mother bear with her two cubs came into camp. One cub walked on Jack's arm, and when he moved his arm, the cub bit him. He let out another cry for help and by then all the dudes were awake and frightened. We gathered up more wood and built a roaring fire. I also turned the spotlight from the truck on the campground; but in spite of all, when daylight came, we saw the old mother bear sitting in front of Helen Deering's tent. There was nothing we could do to get that mother bear to move. We saw one of the cubs in a tree just above the tent, so we told Helen to stay put and she would be safe. The rest of us ate breakfast, but it was 10 o'clock before the bear finally decided to move on and a shaky Helen could come out of her tent."

The dudes liked wild animals. There was always excitement when deer, moose or elk came into sight. Singing birds and squawking camp robbers were everywhere.

Sometimes pack trips were planned for other parts of the Absoraka range. Trails wound back and forth along the mountainside, but guides could always find a little meadow where horses could graze and with a place flat enough for camp. Wood was plentiful and practically all cooking was done over an open camp fire. Sun-up on a typical day found Clyde and Jack bringing in the horses and Bess cooking breakfast for the dudes and the crew while Clyde made sandwiches for the noon-day meal and Jack threw saddles on the horses. Before the dudes came to breakfast, they put their gear outside the flap of their tent, and by the time they had finished eating, packs were in place and the guides were ready to leave. Bess rode the lead horse and Jack was the last man in the string. That way he was aware of any difficulty with rider or pack. Clyde and another packer, very often Bill, took a short cut to the next campsite to get it set up and ready for dudes when they arrived in the evening.

There were a few psychological problems, too. On one of the trips, a 17-year-old girl from a "fine family" in Pennsylvania fell madly in love with Bill. She started following him around. "She was absolutely nuts about him," says Clyde, "and after a few 'goings on,' I called Bill over and had a good talk with him. I told him to ignore her and not to leave camp with her at any time, reminding him we were responsible for her and also for his actions.

"Then there was the old maid who fell for me. Wherever I went, she would follow. I could hardly get away from her even to go to the brush. I finally asked Bess to help with the problem. That made for a lot of fun in camp and I took a heap of kidding. On the trail I made a point of riding with Bess, if possible. One day we were headed for West Thumb of Yellowstone Lake with me leading out. A deer came in sight and most of the dudes stopped to watch. I rode on and when I looked back, there was Lulu Belle close behind me. We were crowding our horses down a narrow trail that had just been cleared and there were little stumps sticking up from the ground. Lulu's horse stumbled and she went flying over his head. I got off my horse and went to her. Only her pride was wounded, so I picked up her shoes and gave them to her with strict instructions to stay with the rest of the party. She still wouldn't let me out of her sight.

"Two days later we were heading for the outlet of Yellowstone Lake; the trail was washed out in places by spring floods and the ditches were three feet deep and five to six feet wide. I always told dudes not to stop and water their horses unless I stopped to water mine, since I had to keep the riders together. I was leading out, with Lulu Belle right behind. I crossed one of the ditches and when she got there, her horse wanted a drink. She remembered my instructions and jerked his head up so suddenly that he went over backwards, landing Lulu Belle in the water. Her horse got to his feet and pulled out, leaving her behind. Bess yelled, 'Clyde, come help her out.' So I did; I got off my horse and bent down to rescue Lulu. I was all dressed up for the Yellowstone — big Western hat, curly chaps, polished boots and a new pink silk shirt. Well, Lulu Belle was a big gal, about 190 pounds, and stood six foot three. When I took hold of her hands, she pulled me right on top of her into the mud and water. Everyone roared with laughter. We finally got Lulu back on her horse and rode two miles to a spring where we had planned a picnic lunch. Lulu got cleaned up there and went behind a bush to put on a slicker. After lunch we all wanted a good drink of spring water and lay down to drink horse fashion. I'll be darned if Lulu Belle didn't fall in the water again. This time we just let her dry out as she rode along. I was relieved when Lulu Belle headed East."

* * *

The biggest pack trip ever organized by the OTO was the one sponsored by the Sierra Club of San Francisco, and was joined for the Yellowstone trip by members of the Prairie Hiking Club of the Mid-west and by the Appalachian Club from the East coast. There were 368 members who made the trip.

Mr. Colby, head of the Sierra Club, had contacted Mr. Albright, superintendent of the Park asking about a guide for their proposed trip. Mr. Albright recommended Dick Randall, but Dick was tied up with the Dodge party that summer, and it was decided that Clyde Erskine would manage the trip. The Sierra Club would plan for the food, bring a cook and his assistants. They needed guides and pack horses. Eighteen guests needed horses to ride; the rest planned to walk.

Clyde calculated it would take over 100 horses for the trip and that many could not be spared from regular activities at the OTO. He went to Hardin, Montana, and bought 70 head of pack horses. Packs and other equipment had to be secured for all of them and a crew hired. Following is Clyde's first hand account of those preparations and the trip:

> We unloaded those horses at the train station at Carbella and trailed them 18 miles to the ranch. Two men were assigned to herd them until we were ready to start on the trip. I had just finished building the large log saddle barn and a corral. All these

horses had to be shod. We advertised for experienced packers who knew how to tie a Diamond hitch and seventy-five men showed up for a tryout. I found that some couldn't even tie a shoe lace, much less a Diamond Hitch capable of holding a pack in place. Thank the Lord, I did have three old-time cowboys who could handle a rope; these men could lasso anything that moved. We also found that many of the new horses had never been packed, so we had to break them to that.

In order to get such a huge party organized, I divided it into units of two men and ten horses each. The first Unit was called "A," and a huge A was painted on every horse, every saddle and packsack that was part of that unit. Then each individual horse and its equipment was given a number, so we had A-1 on that horse, saddle, bridle and pack. The next horse and his equipment was A-2 and so on up to ten. The second unit was lettered B and numbered the same way. With this system, when pulling into camp at night a guide could quickly tell if any horse was missing. I hired 23 men to help on the trip and required each one to sign a contract stating he would not leave the outfit during the course of the trip except for extreme emergency. Packers and guides were to be paid at the end of the trip and only if they had completed it. That contract saved me a lot of grief, and we lost only one packer.

The Sierra Club members came by train to West Yellowstone and we met them at Old Faithful Inn on July 14, 1926. There was Mr. Colby with 367 other Sierra Club members, all eager to start for this back country. We had 80 pack horses and 16 packers to handle the luggage. Ten mules were included for packing kitchen equipment and supplies and two men had charge of that operation. There were 18 saddle horses for those guests who needed to ride and 24 for our crew. Besides packers, we had two night-herders and two wranglers. That meant 126 animals and 392 people to be cared for and accounted for in wilderness high-country with few trails or markers.

I rode in front to head out the string; the chief packer kept riding up and down the string checking packs and horses. When we made camp each night, all my men had a job to do as horses were unpacked and checked in by number. Each night we put up a rope corral for the horses. In the morning the trail boss called off the number of each horse as it was caught and the two men in charge of that unit would get the pack saddle with the same number and saddle as the animal. This was important because each saddle and pack had been fitted and adjusted to each individual horse before the trip began. Each pack horse carried five duffle bags weighing 32 pounds each. They were weighed and checked out every morning before being put on the horses.

The mules carried three large cook stoves and it took a good packer to throw a double Diamond Hitch over that load and make it balance. Judge Tappan of Los Angeles was the head cook and he had 20 other Sierra Club members as cook's helpers. On most mornings, we had breakfast finished, the horses packed and were on the trail by 8 a.m. Kitchen equipment was sent ahead so the kitchen crew could get it set up for the evening meal. Anyone wanting to eat at noon put up a lunch for himself after we finished breakfast.

We were out over two weeks and had only one bad day. This was when we were crossing the Continental Divide between the lower part of Shoshone Lake and the road leading to Jackson Hole. We stopped at an old Yellowstone Park campground. Immediately, horse flies descended in swarms. It was before the days of insect repellants. Horses rubbed against the trees and bucked around so much fighting flies that pack saddles were loosened and swung around to the horses' bellies. Some broke loose from the string and our three ropers were kept busy catching the harassed animals. It took six men a long time to get packs back in place. One of the wranglers and I had gone ahead into thick timber with about 40 head of horses and we were attacked by another swarm of flies. We all got into camp about 3 p.m., thankful we were out of that mess, when I began to hear, "I can't find my duffle bag." We checked the string and found 40 bags and 8 pack horses missing. Missing, too, was Candy, our little mascot and two broncs we used to entertain with. Henry, my head packer, and six other men went back over the trail to catch the pack horses before they got headed for home. The men were out all night, but came in the next morning with all missing horses and every one of the 40 bags.

Mr. Colby was upset about the horse flies and missing duffle bags and said he was going to call the trip off. I said, "Mr. Colby, I've been in the mountains a long time and that is the worst I have ever seen horse flies; it was just too much for the horses to take. I have a contract with you and I intend to fill it to the best of my ability and finish the trip."

From that day on, everything went like clockwork. During the last part of the trip, we rode around the east end of Yellowstone Lake and then, for three days, camped at the foot of Mt. Sheridan. We had made arrangements ahead of time to have a boat bring food to that designated spot and cache it in one of the ranger's snowshoe cabins, so it would be safe from bears. That gave us all a treat of fresh food.

On the 16th day of the trip, Bess and the Governor came to the Canyon and met us. They settled accounts with Mr. Colby and the wranglers. We completed the trip with no accident or loss of horse or equipment. 368 tired but happy Sierra Club members boarded the train at West Yellowstone for the return trip to their homes. Packs and saddles were loaded on a truck and taken back to the OTO. Four wranglers trailed the horses to the ranch, they could travel fast with no packs, and when they were headed for home pasture.

I was exhausted, but gratified when Mr. Colby wrote us a letter saying it was the best and most pleasant trip they had ever taken. They especially appreciated the courteous crew and efficient organization; that pleased me.

Before Bess and I left the Park after the Sierra Club trip Max Goodsell, general passenger agent of the Northern Pacific, said that Miss Amy Onken, president of Pi Beta Phi wanted to make arrangements to hold a national convention in the Park the next summer. Bess was appointed convention guide, coordinated all preliminary plans, and served as official hostess for 500 sorority girls when they came in 1927. The Pi Phis completely filled Old Faithful Lodge and Inn.

Clyde took charge of serving the banquet for the convention, a decided contrast in menu and service to the meals on that big pack trip. Once again the members of this remarkable family proved their skill in organization and handling people, able to manage a mountain pack trip or a sorority convention with equal ease and graciousness.

DUDE RANCHING
MAKES THE HEADLINES

National magazines were publishing articles about dude ranching. Early in 1925, J. C. Dockarty wrote one for *Motor Life* and in it explained that "in the language of the cow country, a 'dude' is a summer visitor who is more or less unfamiliar with the ways of ranching. The 'dude' ranches of Montana and Wyoming are not movie set ups but real cow ranches with comforts and accommodations for summer visitors. A horse wrangler is a man who cares for the ranch string of ponies, seeing that they have rest, water, and pasturage. By evolution a 'dude wrangler' is one who performs the same function for 'dudes.'...On most of the dude ranches the daily work of line-riding, herding and chores continues as of old with the exception that the visitor has an opportunity to observe and he or she has a chance to participate in the romance of the range and corral. That 'she' pronoun...didn't just sneak in; it belongs here...girls and women make just as worthy dudes as do their menfolk."

Mr. Dockarty's statements and some by Katherine Courtland were used as a basis for an article in the "Sports and Athletics" section of the June 27, 1925 issue of *The Literary Digest*.

Katherine Simons Courtland was an early-day guest at the OTO Ranch and went on one of the horseback trips around Yellowstone Park. Later she wrote an article for *The World Traveler* which she entitled "A Lady on a Dude Ranch." It was illustrated with a picture of Bess Randall Erskine on her horse and with an OTO camp photo. The article gave a "dude's eye view" of these vacations. The following quotations are part of those reprinted by *Literary Digest* and the "lady from Boston" was also a guest at the OTO.

"When some rip-snorting, stiff-legged steam engine of a horse at a western rodeo tries to throw a debonair, grinning dare-devil of a rider, the cow punchers hanging on the fence roar out an old familiar exhortation. 'Ride 'im cowboy!'

"This well known cry seems to make the careening rider stick tighter than ever, but I know it never brings to the heart of any buckaroo the thrill of pride and joy it can bring to a lady like the Lady from Boston whom I watched one morning from the front porch of a certain ranch in old Montana.

"She came galloping down the canyon road, boots firmly pressed against the strong sides of a fast Montana cayuse, stray locks of hair streaming back under a rakish Stetson, gay yellow kerchief blowing in the wind! A group of wranglers, bringing up a bunch of horses from the lower corral, halted on the edge of the timber to give her the road.

" 'Ride 'im cowboy!' they shouted, waving their hats high as she galloped past, and I saw the flash of her joyous smile as she answered the greeting with a quick, free lift of her right arm that looked like she was trying to touch the sky all in one motion. The picture came back to me when I mentioned the title of this article to a dude ranching friend of mine. He murmered, 'A Lady on a Dude Ranch..When is a lady more than a lady?' and then answered the question, 'When she is on a dude ranch!'

"I am thinking not only of the Lady from Boston, but of all other women from grandmothers down to flappers whom I have observed during their introduction to ranch life. I cannot think of a single one who did not leave the ranch a more interesting person then when she arrived. That applies not alone to women, of course. It is true of all 'dudes.' A summer at a dude ranch does something to you, from which you never quite recover....

"Confirmed dudes go to Wyoming and Montana summer after summer from nearly every state in the Union...Some of them choose dude ranches on the plains of the cattle country' others seek out mountain ranches up in the Rockies....Usually they have one favorite spot which they always refer to as 'the ranch' or even as 'my ranch.'

"I suppose most of the confirmed dudes are men, but I doubt if the men dudes are ever greater enthusiasts then the women. Sometimes I wonder if anyone could enjoy anything more than the average American girl enjoys her first taste of dude ranch life. Not just girls either. I could tell you about a white-haired grandmother and a certain prized pony, but the Lady from Boston is a good example.

"I knew from the moment I saw her response to the wranglers' greeting that she, too, was a confirmed dude, and she admitted it to me that evening. We stood in front of her little log cabin on the edge of the forest saying good night after an hilarious evening before the ranch fireplace. Strains of piano and banjo music were still coming from the house, where the dancing and singing would continue for half an hour longer. The moon was fantastically large and as white as a snowy owl in the black sky. A flock of drifting clouds cast great shadows upon the mountains and valleys extending above and below us. Snow gleamed in the moonlight on the tops of the highest peaks and I caught the glint of the silver light where it touched the lake down at the foot of Lookout Mountain.

"Standing silent for a long moment, we listened to the night sounds — wind in the top of the pines, the melodious rush of Cedar Creek in its ceaseless tumble down the side of the mountain just behind our cabins, the sleepy call of a bird, a whinny from the distant corral, and yes, there it came, the shivery howl of a coyote over on Hard Luck Ridge.

" 'I'm coming back next year,' said the Lady solemnly with almost the tone one uses in taking an oath 'and the next year, and the next year, and the next until I die.'

" 'Why do you want to come back?' I asked her knowing what the answer would be, but wishing to hear her version of it.

" 'I can't tell you all in one sentence, of course,' she answered, 'but mostly I think it is this—I'm a different person since I came out here.'

They sat down on the little split log step and continued to talk.

" 'When I came out I didn't know anything about dude

ranches except they were a rather new type of western resort.... I came because I wanted to know the Rockies and I had to stay some place while I made their acquaintances.

" 'Of course, I had an inferiority complex, too, fed by magazine stories of hardened westerners and timid tenderfeet. I expected to be sadly embarrassed by my ignorance of ranch life and things western. But as you know, all that is soon changed.

" 'My first big surprise was the discovery that a dude ranch is a regular ranch — that the term 'dude' is a perfectly respectful western name for strangers from the city to distinguish them from the seasoned old-timers. I found out that the only difference between this ranch and the one across the ridge which bears no title of 'dude' is the fact that there's more work to be done over here — haying and cattle raising and keeping a flock of eastern guests happy and comfortable all at the same time.'

" 'When did you begin to feel at home?' I asked her.

" 'Immediately,' she replied. 'How do these Montana folks do it? When they welcome new-comers to the ranch they give us the feeling that the entire outfit has been only existing up to the moment of our arrival and that life from now on is to be the real thing. It is the warmest, most natural welcome I have ever had.' "

During her stay at the ranch, the Lady from Boston went with Bess one day when Dick sent her out to buy some horses. They stopped at Ted Anderson's ranch because he had a horse he wanted to sell. Bess looked the mare over carefully and said, "How much you holding her for?"

"Hundred sixty."

"She's not worth that much." Bess said from her perch in the saddle. "Give you forty."

"O.K." said Anderson and handed her the halter rope. Bess paid for the horse and rode off leading it down the trail.

"You can always return the horse if you don't like it and get your money back," suggested the Lady from Boston, "we do that at our stores in the East."

"Can't do it here," Bess told her. "A horse trade is a horse trade and it's final. Dick Randall had always taught her that a handshake is as binding as a signed document. "If a man's word ain't good, his paper ain't." he often said.

Bess had noticed some blemishes on the mare, but she could also see that the horse was gentle and well built.

"If she proves to be too rough for riding," Bess assured her friend, "we can put her in the pack string." And the Lady from Boston learned that once you buy a horse, good or bad, it's yours to keep.

NOT A SPOILED BRAT LEFT

The ranch buildings were in good shape and adequate for a large number of guests; and hired cowboys could take care of the winter work. To make a dude ranch successful, there had to be a full booking of guests for the all-too-short Montana summers. Dick and Mother Randall went East each winter, and the Erskines began to contact people on the West Coast. They found that resort hotels in California were open and needed managers in winter months when the OTO was closed. They began managing resorts like the one at Lake Arrowhead during the OTO off-season and they often met people there who were interested in a summer dude ranch vacation.

Through one of these California connections, Clyde booked a party of boys from Pasadena Junior College for the summer of 1929. Clyde recalls:

> While I was at Lake Arrowhead, I got in touch with Mr. Loucas, a professor at Pasadena Junior College. We arranged for him to bring a party of boys for a fifteen-day stay in Montana the next summer. By May, he had sixteen boys, ages fifteen to eighteen, booked for the summer and he was to come with them.
>
> I met the group in July at West Yellowstone and drove them to our OTO Ranch. We assigned the boys to the lower floor of the dormitory. During the next few days, we were busy preparing horses, saddles, and the boys for the trip. We put together an outfit for each boy that would be most suitable for him.
>
> I can't remember all their names, but they were a fine group of boys and six, especially, stay in my memory: Don Douglas of the Douglas Aircraft family; a Northrup boy from the Northrup Airplane Company, and a Palmer boy from the fountain pen company. Horace Lagmar was a cousin of Palmer's. There were

also Tom Warner of the Steward-Warner Company and Scotty Armstrong whose father was head of a chain of banks on the Pacific coast.

The boys were to be with us for 45 days; we planned a two week camping trip into rugged mountain country and the rest of the time would be spent at the OTO ranch and camps. It took three days to get horses assigned, equipment lined up, and the boys acquainted with their horses. All of the boys had ridden before, so that was no problem. Mr. Loucas was a fine leader and handled the group well. They were eager to hit the trail.

I led off as guide and behind me on the narrow trail came our seventeen guests on horseback. Bess came along as chief cook. There were also ten packhorses and my off-side packer, for bringing up the rear and seeing that packs and horses stayed in order. The trail wound up Cedar Creek fourteen miles to the top of the Continental Divide, then along Mill Creek and Horse Creek. From the Divide we could look south and see Yellowstone Lake and the Grand Teton Mountains. The California boys had fun playing in the glacial snowbanks.

We arrived at crystal-clear Knox Lake about 4 p.m. on the first day of our ride. I told the boys to unsaddle their horses and tie each to a different tree and that I would come along and put the hobbles on. The boys put up their tents as the packer and I unloaded them from packhorses. They gathered pine boughs for beds and spread out their bed rolls. We turned the horses out into the meadow for the night. I got camp set up, so Bess could cook supper for the hungry crew. I asked if there were any volunteers to help her and four boys jumped up immediately. I took the rest to get wood for a bonfire. We spread out over the hillside and I rode a horse so we could snake in the big pieces. That was the first of many happy bonfires and evenings of stories and songs.

Next morning the boys took their fishing rods down to the lake and by the time Bess had breakfast ready, each had his limit. I showed them how to clean fish and every one got a kick out of getting the fish ready for the frying pan. Bess fried the fish and made pancakes. When Horace Lagmar said he didn't like pancakes, Bess said, "What! Have you ever had a real flapjack cooked on a camp stove?" He admitted he had never tried any kind of pancake, so Bess fixed a couple for him, hot and covered with ranch butter and Log Cabin syrup. We soon had a convert, and before the meal was over, Horace had eaten two brook trout and eight pancakes.

We built a smoke house and taught the boys how to smoke fish. When we all had a good fill of fried trout, I asked the boys to bring me their equipment and I filed the barbs off their fish-hooks, explaining that this way they could return to the water any fish caught above the ones needed for eating. They learned how to wet their hands and handle a fish so it would not be harmed. We ate trout once a day during the two weeks we camped at Knox Lake.

**

The time spent camping with those boys and Mr. Loucas was a real joy, and lasting friendships were formed. Twenty years later, Bess and I were guests of some friends of ours at the Lake Frontier Hotel in Las Vegas, Nevada, for dinner one evening. Captain Derian, a partner in an aviation training school in Boulder City, Nevada, came over to our table. I was at that time general manager of the Grand Canyon Boulder Dam Tours at Boulder City and we had a school based at our hanger in Boulder City. All rates had to be approved by the Park Service. "Clyde," he said, "I'm having trouble with the man running that aviation school out of Las Vegas. He wants to raise the rates and I told him that all rates were set by the Park Service."

"What's his name?" I asked.

"Tom Warner," Captain Derian said. "I sure wish you'd come over to his table and talk to him."

I said, "Bring Tom over here, and I'll talk to him." So here came Tom and rather gruffly, he said, "Who are you?"

"You're going to be surprised...take a good look, do you know me?"

"No," and he was becoming more gruff at every question.

"Did you ever see this lady?" and I pointed to Bess.

"No." The executive was clearly not interested in playing games.

So I said, "Do you remember Bess and Clyde at Knox Lake and the OTO Ranch?" With that Tom Warner threw his arms around me and then around Bess. He hurried over to his table and brought his wife to meet us. We spent the rest of the evening remembering that trip in the mountains. He admitted he had been pretty much a spoiled brat, but he treasured the expeiences of that trip more than any other in his life.

***

We had said good-bye to the Pasadena boys and were settling back to relax for the rest of the day, thankful the vacation with the boys had gone so well and that not one of them had been hurt. We felt like celebrating, so had a round of cocktails and then headed for the dining room. We no more than sat down at the table when we heard a strange roar. I rushed to the door and looked out. Peaceful little Cedar Creek was a rampaging river. Water was everywhere. The two-story log bunkhouse had been washed up and was teetering on the bridge. Crests of muddy water rose in the air to ten and twelve feet; big logs were floating downstream or being wedged behind the bunkhouse.

The wranglers ran to the barn and let all livestock out of the buildings and the corrals. The men waded in water up to their waists but managed to open the gates and free the horses. The animals took off for higher ground and not a one was lost. Doors to the saddle room were closed so equipment could not float away but the pack outfit that had been laid out for Dick's next trip was already in the swirling water.

It was a terrible mess, and we had a house full of dudes.

Heavy spring rains and fast melting snow sent down more water than the creek banks could carry. We knew the good road we had worked so hard to build would be washed away and with it the seventeen pole bridges that had provided easy access to the ranch. The old road was on higher ground but had not been used or repaired for two years. We knew we had to get the dudes out.

Cedar Creek, with water fresh from the mountain glaciers, rushed by the OTO cabins.

Heading for the Hell Roaring country. Dick insisted
that a month in the mountains could cure all city ills. —UM

Clyde Erskine wearing the "unborn calfskin" vest made for him by Mother Randall. (1923)

*The dudes, young and old, spent hours practicing on this saw horse.
Many became proficient ropers. Photo courtesy of George Randall.*

Marshall and Stanley Goodsill whose father was General Passenger Agent for the Northern Pacific Railroad and instrumental in organizing the Dude Ranch Association. He sent his sons to the OTO so Dick could teach them how to ride. Taken in 1925.

Dick in the opening to Castle Caves views the cliffs beyond the valleys on his ranch.

Miss Jane Gray of Ohio and her ranch horse Nibs. Angora chaps were tops in style.

Next best to horseback riding, the Governor recommended mountain climbing.

A morning ride into the High Country. —UM

Glacier fun, elevation 10,000 feet. —UM

*1929. We met the Pasadena boys at the train station in West Yellowstone.
They rode to the ranch in the OTO truck.*

Bess and Clyde Erskine and some of the Pasadena boys in camp.

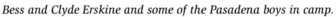

Pasadena boys swimming in Knox Lake.

*It isn't hard to "go Western" when
a handsome Wrangler plays the guitar.*

The dining room at the OTO.

Dick Randall loved to entertain and had his horse, Duke, trained for performances.

Clyde and Bess at the Wigwam Resort near Phoenix which they managed for three seasons in the 30s. The resort was owned by Goodyear Tire and Rubber Company. —Museum of the Rockies

Yellowstone Chip (Samuelson), head wrangler for several years at the OTO, strums his guitar and sings for the dudes gathered on the steps of the lodge.
—Museum of the Rockies

Every good wrangler could roll his own and teach the dudes how to do it, too. Photo courtesy of George Randall.

A 16 day saddle horse trip through Yellowstone on the Howard Eaton trail. Teepees had to be set up at every stop and packed again in the morning. Bess was the official camp cook. —UM

Dude Ranchers convention at the Northern Hotel in Billings in 1930.

By 1902 the buffalo had disappeared from the Montana plains but a herd in the park was carefully cared for to preserve the species. Each year a buffalo roundup was held at Soda Butte.

Sunset.

Dick and Mother Randall's 60th anniversary picture.

It was our only hope.

The power house was flooded; all power and water lines went out of commission immediately, but all guests were in the big lodge and safe.

By morning the water had receded and all hands, dudes included, set to work repairing the old road so we could get cars over it. Six cars belonging to the dudes were on high ground and had escaped the flood, and these were used to take people out. I drove each car out and had two of our wranglers stand on the running boards to keep the car from toppling over. At best the road was narrow and rough and wound precariously along the side of the mountain; now it was wet and slick from the rain.

Our Japanese cook was terrified. He and his helper packed their belongings in a sack and begged me to take them out, too. I assured them the water would get no higher and there was no real danger, so they reluctantly remained to help us clean up the mess. The place was in shambles; the bunkhouse destroyed beyond repair. We rescued what logs we could and later sawed them up for firewood.

We were thankful that we had gotten every dude out safely, but it was early summer and our whole season was ruined. It was a terrible financial loss; we had to cancel all reservations for that year. The property damage was devastating, but not a single person or animal had been injured.

Our loyal OTO dudes started right in making reservations for the next year. We were faced with a tremendous clean-up and repair job, but we knew the OTO would go on.

* * *

Sometimes our problems were man made, like the time the Governor arrived at Hell Roaring camp with a large party of hunters in bitter cold weather and found no wood in the cabin.

Charlie and Ora Ritchie had been coming to the OTO for several seasons, usually staying a month. They decided they wanted Bess and me to take them on a long hunting and pack trip into the Hell Roaring country. We set the time for August 15 to September 15. Dr. Mead, from New Brighton, Pennsylvania, who was often our guest at the ranch, joined us. That made a party of five plus Bill Watson, my side packer. We went up Cedar Creek across the Divide and down to Knox Lake where we stayed three days, then on to Hell Roaring Camp. The Governor had built the hunting cabin there in 1911 and it was a favorite place with all our dudes.

There was now a ranger station about half a mile from it and the forest service men were building a fence at the time we arrived, and came to visit us. One of the workers went back to the ranger station and made hot biscuits for our supper. They were delicious, but we didn't realize how dearly we were to pay for those "forest service biscuits."

We stayed at Hell Roaring for five or six days and fished the country within a radius of several miles. The fishing in Hell Roaring creek, where it joined the Yellowstone, was superb.

While we were in camp, I had Bill bring in about half a cord of stove wood so it would be dry and ready for the Governor when he brought his elk hunting party in that fall. I knew how tough it was to get to a winter camp and not have dry wood, especially if you had some dudes along, so we left everything in readiness. I even laid a fire in the cook stove and put a tin of matches there, so if the hunters came in with fingers stiff from the cold, they could get a fire going right away. We closed up the cabin and left, knowing no one else was scheduled to be there until hunting season.

It was late October when Dick took his hunting party out and headed for the Hell Roaring camp. The snow was deep, and the storm was bringing the elk down from the high country summer pasture. "I was having a hell of a time with those city dudes; they weren't used to mountain conditions or winter weather," Dick told us later. "The storm was bad and we were soaking wet and just about worn out when we rode into Hell Roaring. I'd sort of kept their spirits up promisin' that as soon as we reached the cabin, we could get a fire going, dry out and have a hot meal. When I got inside the cabin, I saw there wasn't a single stick of wood. The snow was three feet deep on the level outside. My packer and I started digging through it hoping to find some wood we could use. I got madder with every shovel full of snow. Why wasn't there any wood in the cabin? We finally managed to get pine boughs and pitch enough to build a fire. The dudes were cold, hungry and cross. I kept wondering what in hell had happened to the wood Clyde had left for us."

The Governor was still fuming when he got back to the ranch with his hunters. Later, I met up with Frenchy, one of the men who had been working on the fence and asked if he knew what had happened to the wood. He said, "Sure, that damned forest ranger did it. I tried to tell him it was wrong to take wood out of a cabin and that the Governor would be coming in with a hunting party and need that dry wood. But I couldn't stop him."

The next spring I was working on building seventeen miles of new road into the ranch. One day, I looked up and here came that ranger down the trail. It made me so damn mad just to see him that I wanted to pull him down out of the saddle and knock the hell out of him.

He said, "Hello."

I said, "I suppose you kept cozy this winter with the wood you took out of Hell Roaring camp." Then I changed my tone and said, "Now, I'm telling you, get out of my sight and if I ever meet you where we have witnesses, I will beat the hell out of you!" I have never seen him since.

There are some unwritten laws in the West that newcomers have to learn — like horse trading; a man's word is as good as his signature; and you don't take wood out of a mountain cabin.

BE PREPARED
FOR THE UNEXPECTED

No dude ranch story would be complete without something about the cooks. They were an important part of dude ranching both at the OTO home place and in the mountains. There were tall ones and short ones, men and women; they had Chinese and Japanese cooks, good ones and bad ones. With all of this and throughout the years, Mother Randall and Bess often found themselves back in the kitchen when one of the cooks decided to leave or go on a spree.

The OTO had a Chinese cook that insisted on cooking the lettuce. Twice a day, he took the choice heads, cut them up and boiled them. Mother Randall tried to hide the lettuce from him, but every day he managed to find and cook some lettuce. Cooks were hard to get, but Mother Randall finally had to fire him and get someone who would serve lettuce as a salad. Clyde continues:

Then we had a big tall white cook, mean looking and sullen. About the second night he served mashed potatoes so soggy and watery you couldn't eat them. Mother knew something had to be done. She also knew better than to go into the kitchen in the middle of serving dinner, so she waited until the meal was over to talk to him. She told him as tactfully as possible that the potatoes would have to be prepared differently and suggested how it could be done. He yanked off his apron, said if she knew how to do it, she could take over, and he left. There we were with 75 guests and no cook. Mother Randall, as always, took over until we would get another.

Our Japanese crew was great. The chef, William, had been Cecil B. deMille's chef in Los Angeles at one time. I had brought him to the ranch from Lake Arrowhead where he had cooked for us during the winter months. The summer he was at the OTO was a joy for all of us and things went smoothly in the kitchen and dining room. We did find the chef was cutting only choice pieces from the young steers we were butchering and throwing the rest of the meat in the garbage. He could do that with deMille, but we couldn't afford it, and so convinced him that the lesser cuts could be used, too. After he understood the situation, it was O.K. with him and he used all the meat. That winter he was killed in a traffic accident in Los Angeles. We felt we had lost a real friend.

But we continued to have Japanese cooks. The next was Okie who was a good cook, but we found large sacks of rice were disappearing too fast. Upon investigating, we discovered the kitchen crew was making saki in the basement. We ordered all their saki thrown down the sink. They were angry and threatened to quit but finally decided to finish the summer since I had promised to take them back to California with us in the fall.

One woman cook could turn out fine food, but she was so fond of beer that sometimes she couldn't cook. We found she was making her own beer in the basement in a large crock that we ordinarily used for putting down spiced apples. We had a big two-oven cook stove fueled with wood. One evening when it was time to serve dinner, the waitresses went to the kitchen only to find that the cook hadn't started dinner. She was frantically throwing wood out of the woodbox hunting for a mouse that she had seen go in. She said she wasn't going to cook dinner until she got rid of that mouse. Between the beer and the mouse, we had to let her go, and Mother Randall took over until we could find a replacement.

One summer after a cook quit, our guest Colonel Knox of Corpus Christie came to our rescue. He had brought with him a colored quartermaster who had cooked for the Colonel in the army. He had graduated from a cooking school, was capable and refined and respected by all of us. He was great and we all appreciated his food and his willingness to help. Even Colonel Knox tried to lend a hand but after one fiasco cooking rice and discovering too late how much it swelled, he left the cooking to the quartermaster. Dick came in one day from an exploration trip in the high country and said to the cook, "I've been making maps and naming some areas and I named one mountain after you."

The young man was surprised and said "What did you call it?"

"Niggerhead Peak," said Dick. The quartermaster laughed and was pleased to have the recognition. This was many years ago. Dick Randall meant no offense and the young man took none. "Niggerhead Peak" can still be found on maps of the Absoraka mountain range.

Once we had a Chinese cook with us on one of the pack trips. He was a good camp cook and willing to put up with most inconveniences, but the night a bear walked over him and blew his breath in Woon's face was too much. We could hear him yelling all over camp. He had awakened to find a bear, not only in his tent but right on top of him. Woon scrambled out of the tent and climbed the nearest tree. We couldn't get him to come down until the bear had been sent well on his way back into the timber. When Woon did come down, he was still shaking. "More bear; no more cookie," he declared in no uncertain terms, so we had to send a wrangler back to the ranch with Woon, and Dick took over the cooking. The Governor was a wonderful camp cook. He could turn out mouth-watering biscuits in a dutch oven over a camp fire, and cook mountain trout to perfection. In fact, there were few things the Governor couldn't do if he set his mind to it.

Our dude friends, who were becoming more and more a part of the extended OTO family, often helped us with the work. Sometimes even newcomers lent a hand, like the fall when we were getting in the potatoes. The Governor was out with Vinson and a hunting party when Mother Randall got word her father had died. Her son, Gay, drove her to St. Anthony, Idaho, for the funeral. That left Bess, Old Charlie, and me to get the potato crop in. It was getting late in the season and storms were reported coming our way. We had George Richard, Gay's five year old son with us.

Old Charlie, the choreboy, was a bit "touched in the head" but he could run the plow. The trouble was he plowed up too many potatoes at a time and we couldn't keep up with him; nor could we get him to stop. There we were with the year's supply of potatoes out on the ground and a storm coming in. We built a sagebrush fire to keep little Richard warm while Bess and I worked frantically to get the potatoes picked up and put in sacks. It was about 4 o'clock in the afternoon; we were dead tired and still had all the chores to do when we finished the potatoes. We looked up and saw two men coming down the road toward us. Guests were the last thing we wanted at that moment. The men wanted to go on a hunting trip with Dick Randall but had not made any arrangements ahead of time. They would also like to spend some time at the ranch. We told them we would try to arrange it, but right now we had to get the potato crop in and suggested they go back to the Lodge and wait for us. Those two strangers from California looked up and down the rows of uncovered potatoes, sized up the situation, and pitched in to help. One was Mr. Sharples who had introduced avacados into California; he had brought some plants from Hawaii and started raising them at Santa Anna. They were huge avacados and he shipped them to New York and sold them for one dollar each. The other man was Mr. Perkins, a rose specialist.

With all of us working, we finished getting in the potatoes about ten o'clock that night. When they were safely in the root cellar, I went out to help Charlie with the chores while Bess got supper.

People were our livelihood and we did genuinely enjoy them, not only as paying guests, but as friends. Occasionally we longed for a day when we could be alone and not responsible for anyone else's welfare....like the day after the potato picking. It was Sunday and promised to be a quiet one with only the two men from California as guests. But about 11 o'clock in came two carloads of people. Bess calculated that would make sixteen for dinner, so the two chickens in the pot wouldn't go around. She and Charlie hurriedly caught and dressed six more chickens. Dinner was delicious, always, with fried chicken, hot biscuits, gravy, and chocolate cake for dessert.

Just as we finished dinner, Dick came in with his hunting party, so they had to be fed, too. This was typical of dude ranching. We had to be prepared for the unexpected. We had no telephone for problem solving in those days, so last minute guests couldn't call head for reservations; they just dropped by for a meal or a week.

* * *

The Governor loved to entertain. Sometimes he clowned around, pretending to be a new dude getting on a horse. He would come out dressed in golf knickers, rattlesnake socks, and cap. With great gusto he jumped up on the horse from the wrong side and landed back of the saddle facing the horse's tail. Sometimes he jumped clear over the horse and landed in the dirt on the other side. Often the wranglers helped him with these performances and they always brought a laugh from the dudes. Dick had a horse trained to do tricks and many a summer evening found Dick and his horse amusing the guests.

Bess wrote a song for the OTO and the dudes sang it lustily around camp fires, in front of the lodge fireplace, at meals, at rodeos, and even at OTO reunions back East.

> I'm a dude of the OTO
> I'm the wildest thing you know
> I ride the meanest horse
> And fill it with remorse.
> I throw the lariat
> I'm sure to get you yet
> They say that I'm not slow
> I'm a dude of the OTO.

Clyde talks about the entertainment:

One year the Governor bought two truck loads of costumes from a costume dealer in New York and had them shipped to the ranch. Every summer after that we had a big masquerade ball. Guests were turned loose in the costume room and asked to

108

choose what they would like to wear. Some added to the fun by mixing parts of costumes and appearing at the dance in something like a King George coat, a pair of convict trousers and a derby hat. The costume ball became one of the big events at the OTO.

The little boys liked to play rodeo; they "rode" the log fences and roped the fence posts. They rode the Buckaroo and roped the sawhorse animal we had fixed up for practice roping. One day I went up to the calf corral and it seemed to me some of the calves were looking swayback. I guessed what had been going on and later found the little boys, led by the Governor's two grandsons, George and Bill, were going up there every day, roping the calves and riding them. I explained that the little calves' legs and backs weren't strong enough to hold the extra weight...some of the boys were 13 and 14 years old and pretty husky. I knew we would have no steers to butcher for next year's meat if this kept up; the young guernseys fed and fattened on sweet clover made excellent meat.

We brought in some goats for the kids to ride and fixed up another wooden roping horse just for them. The boys were interested in learning how to lasso and spent hours practicing. Some of the dudes, young and not so young, became proficient ropers. Dick was always glad to teach children how to ride and handle a horse properly and kept plenty of gentle horses at the ranch so every child could have his own.

Candy, the little cream-colored horse with OTO markings on his face, had been our mascot on the Sierra Club trip. He was now about eight years old and quite a pet. The Governor gave this horse to his grandson, Bill. But everytime Bill tried to get on Candy, he got bucked off. One day as I was walking toward the Lodge, Candy dumped Bill as they crossed the bridge right in front of me. I said, "I thought you were a cowboy, Bill." He picked himself up from the ground and said, "I am, Uncle Clyde, but I just can't stay on Candy."

"Sure you can," I told him. "You can do anything you make your mind up to do. Now go and get on that horse, and this time you stick tight." That was when Bill really became a cowboy, and some years later he was riding in real rodeos and collecting big prize money.

Entertainment wasn't always planned. There was the time the Governor brought home the chickens. It was in the spring of 1928. Bess and I had just returned from California in our beautiful new Stutz roadster. We were proud of that car; it was the first fancy one we had been able to afford.

Soon after we got to the ranch, the Governor asked me to drive him to Gardiner. He had fun showing off the new car to his friends in town and after three or four hours of shopping, said, "I have only one other place to go. Drive over to Henry Anderson's house." Henry was one of our most responsible and capable packers and an excellent big game hunter and guide. He also raised chickens. We stopped in front of Henry's house and the Governor got out. "I'll only be a minute," he said and disappeared. A few minutes later the Governor and Henry came out with a big crate full of chickens. I was horrified.

"We can't take those chickens in this new car," I protested, but the Governor was not to be stopped.

"Sure we can," he said and proceeded to open the rumble seat and poke the chickens in one by one as Henry handed them to him. By the time they were ready to shut the door we had three dozen squawking chickens flopping around in the car. I was frustrated, but the Governor wasn't. The squawks could be heard for blocks as we left town and headed for home. When we got into the yard at the OTO, the Governor opened the rumble seat and started to take the chickens out. By that time the dudes and wranglers had all come out to see what the noise was about. Chickens and loose feathers flew in all directions and everyone joined in the fun of trying to catch them, and get them into the pen.

When I looked in the rumble seat, I saw that our elegant new Stutz was a mess. It took two years to get that smell and the chicken manure completely cleaned out.

The Governor and Mother Randall continued to go East each winter, as he said again, "You have to take the West to the East to get people interested in coming to a dude ranch." We came to have a large circle of friends from all over the United States. We had guests coming from Pennsylvania, New York, Florida and the New England states, from the West coast and the Mid-west. We loved the dude ranch life and enjoyed the many wonderful people we met. It got to be a very large and close-knit OTO family. Whenever any of us went to the hometown of one of our dudes, we dared not pass them by. They would get busy and have a party for us and introduce us to more of their friends. The business grew, and our bookings were usually filled a year in advance, but we were always careful selecting our guests so they could be congenial and happy together.

Bess and I spent most of our winters managing resort hotels: the Desert Inn at Palm Springs, the Flamingo Hotel in Miami, and for several seasons, the Hotel at Lake Arrowhead in California. While there our friend Mr. Flecker suggested I try out for the movies. He had often heard our evening entertainment when Bess played the piano and I sang. "Clyde," he said, "the moving pictures will be talkies very soon. With a change-over to sound, they are going to need good singers. With your voice, we won't have trouble getting you into the movies. I want to take you up to Hollywood tomorrow to meet a man I have loaned a lot of money to. I think he can place you. The man was Cecil B. deMille. At that time, I had never heard of Cecil B. deMille, but I knew I was just a cowboy from Montana and pretty much a back-woodsman and had no future in a place like Hollywood.

When I told Bess what Mr. Flecker had offered, she asked, "Well, what are you going to do?"

"Well, first off, I can't see myself slobbering over some movie star and still keeping you," I said, "and secondly, we are dude ranchers, are we not?" Bess smiled, agreed, gave me a kiss and for the second time, we concluded we were committed to our life on the OTO, and any entertaining we did would be only for our guests.

COMBINING DUDES WITH COWS

The term "dude" originated in Yellowstone Park, according to Randall, and was first used by early day Park guides. A guest from the East was originally called a "tenderfoot" but gradually that term was replaced by "dude." Ladies were called "dudines" and the children "dudettes," though the latter two terms weren't used extensively, and "dude" became the accepted designation for any guest, man, woman or child. Hosting Eastern visitors on Western ranches became a widespread practice. "Combining dudes with cows," one owner said, "was the best way to make a cattle ranch pay."

"Railroad officials, also vitally interested in this Western vacation idea, thought it would be adventageous if the dude ranchers formed some kind of organization. A.B. Smith, Passenger Traffic Manager of the Northern Pacific Railroad, and Max Goodsill, General Passenger Agent for the railroad, set up a meeting and invited the ranchers to come. The first meeting was held in Bozeman in 1926 and the Dude Ranchers Association was formed. They had begun with a heated discussion about whether the group should be called the Dude Ranchers Association or the Guest Ranchers Association. Dick Randall and the Eatons held out for "dude," saying it was more Western than "guest." They won out and became charter members of the organization and pioneers in the field of dude ranching.

Spike Van Cleve, who with his wife, Barbara, runs the Lazy K Bar Ranch at Big Timber, Montana, looks back over 50 years of dude ranching:

*Dude ranching is an outgrowth of what has always been basic to the West — hospitality....In the heydey of the cattle

---
*"I Am a Dude Rancher" by Spike Van Cleve. DUDE RANCHER, 1976, p. 9.

business, every ranch had a complement of guests from the East, or from abroad...enjoying ranch life; the hunting, fishing, scenery, and ample food. Friends of the owner, friends of friends, mere acquaintances...some stayed a year, and even though the guests could become a damn nuisance, it was over-looked in the name of Western hospitality.

Some of the ranchers began to have second thougts. There was George "Two Dot" Wilson, one of the bigger cattlemen in Central Montana...who was always good for a meal or two, or three, or four, and a place to sleep, so he invariably had a lot of guests, resident as well as grub-line riders.

One evening when there had been a dozen or more outsid-ers for supper and the meal was about over, a rig rattled into the yard. "Two Dot" rose to go the door and his old dog, who had been dozing by the stove, got to his feet and headed for the door, too, wagging his tail enthusiastically.

"Set down, damn you, the old rancher rasped, 'an don't be so all fired friendly. You don't have to feed 'em all. I do."

Other ranchers began to think along the same lines and some of them saw how this here-to-fore free hospitality might be turned into a profit that would keep the ranch afloat when cattle prices wouldn't. So they started charging guests, to their mutual satisfaction."

Dick Randall had combined his hunting parties with the ex-panding homestead he and Dora proved up on in 1898, and de-veloped the OTO, Montana's first dude ranch. He, like most of the dude ranchers that followed, sincerely enjoyed inviting guests into his home, showing them Western country, teaching them to under-stand and appreciate it.

Dude ranching flourished until the Stock Market crash and subsequent depression in the early 1930s. That took its toll; East-erners no longer had money to spend on expensive summer vaca-Some ranches survived and made a comeback when times got better.

Due to the depression, bookings were few at the OTO in 1931, so

Clyde and Bess, who had spent their winters managing resort hotels, took a job managing Yellowstone Park's Old Faithful Inn for that lean summer. Gay Randall and his family were managing the ranch. One of the guests from Boston wanted to buy a ranch and offered a good price for the OTO. Dick and Mother Randall were getting on in years and could no longer keep up the pace they had maintained for so many years as hosts. It was decided to sell the ranch, and for awhile, Bess's brother kept a financial interest in it. Later, that, too, was sold.

Without the Governor's dynamic personality, the OTO lost its following and the new owners turned it back into a full-time stock ranch with no provisions for dudes.

The OTO Dude Ranch enjoyed an enviable position with ranchers and dudes for many years as it pioneered in eveloping Western vacations for Eastern visitors.

The family bought a cattle ranch near Livingston. The Erskines and the Randalls divided their time between that ranch and the winter resort hotels. The Ludwig piano still sits in the ranch parlor and when Bess and Clyde are home for the summer, there is music and song. Sometimes they smile and sing the OTO song just for old times sake.

Dora Roseborough Randall, affectionately called "Mother Randall" by a generation of dudes, lived to be ninety-seven.

James Norris Randall, better known as "Dick" or the "Governor," died on August 20, 1957 after 91 years of a life full of adventure, accomplishment, and love of people. He had guided European royalty and American celebrities; he had entertained people with his stories; he had hosted them at his ranch and taught them to ride horseback. President Theodore Roosevelt gave him a place of honor on the platform during the dedication of Roosevelt Arch at the entrance to Yellowstone Park. The title, "Mr. Dude Rancher," was his without question in the early days of Montana's new industry.

In his last years, Dick Randall found time to write some of his experiences. It is hoped this book will serve to finish the story of his life and adventures as a cowboy, a Yellowstone Park guide, a big game hunter, and a pioneer dude rancher; but most of all, a friend to

people.

Dude ranches and dude ranchers have added a romantic chapter to the history of Montana.

ABOUT THE AUTHORS

Roberta Carkeek Cheney was born and raised on a cattle ranch in southwestern Montana, and though she has lived in many states since, Montana and the ranch house are still home and often the scene of family gatherings.

She has a degree from the University of Montana and has done graduate work in creative writing at Columbia University, Oregon State University and the University of Nevada.

Mrs. Cheney is the author of the book, *Names on the Face of Montana.* She is also coauthor with Emmie Mygatt of three books: *Your Personal Writers' Workshop, This is Wyoming . . . Listen,* and *Hans Kleiber, Artist of the Big Horn Mountains,* a Western Heritage award winner.

Articles by Mrs. Cheney have appeared in *Montana, Magazine of Western History; Montana, Magazine of the Northern Rockies; The Rotarian; True West; Western* (published in Oslo, Norway); *Collector's World; Western Farm Life; Jack & Jill;* and many trade journals and newspapers.

Clyde Erskine was born in Ottumwa, Iowa, on May 12, 1895, and attended Iowa State University. Following his renewed courtship with Helen Elizabeth Randall after the war, he came west, where he was broken in by Dick Randall as a dude wrangler. From his years at the ranch, Clyde Erskine assembled his collection of memoirs, clippings, and photographs for publication.

When the Depression of the early 1930s took its toll of dude ranch reservations, the OTO was sold, and Erskine became manager of resort hotels in California, Arizona, and Florida, often returning to Yellowstone National Park in the summer to manage Old Faithful Inn or the New Mammoth Hotel.